The Digital Photography WORKBOOK

The Digital Photography WORKBOOK

Simon Joinson and Peter Cope

PIATKUS

Printed in Italy by G. Canale & C. S.p.A.

Copyright © 2002 by Simon Joinson and Peter Cope

First published in the UK in 2002
by Judy Piatkus (Publishers) Ltd
5 Windmill Street, London W1T 2JA
e-mail: info@piatkus.co.uk

The moral right of the authors has been asserted

Corel images used by permission

A catalogue record for this book is available from the British Library

ISBN 0 7499 2281 6

Conceived, edited and produced by

Duncan Petersen Publishing, 31 Ceylon Road, London W14 OPY
Designed by Ben Cracknell Studios, 7 St Gregory's Alley, Norwich, Norfolk NR2 1ER
Editorial Director Andrew Duncan
Editor Chris Barstow
Editorial assistant Nicola Davies
Production Sarah Hinks

Contents

Section by section guide

Section by section guide continued

STEP-BY-STEP PROJECTS 4
Montage basics 136

STEP-BY-STEP PROJECTS 5
Fantasy images and fun portraits 152

Beyond image manipulation 190

Introducing digital imaging

Photography reinvented?

What is it that has made digital imaging one of the biggest technological success stories of the past decade, and seen it adopted by people in all walks of life? The answer is that it gives you all the facilities of a well-specified conventional darkroom *and* the opportunity to create powerful new imagery, whether based on photographic realism or visual flights of fantasy. It does so without the need for chemicals or a light-tight room. And in most cases, it does not demand exceptional skills.

But does digital imaging spell the end of conventional photography? No. In the same way that photography itself did not displace painting and other illustrative art forms, so digital imaging provides the means of expanding and enhancing the range of imaging opportunities available to the photographer. This is good news for all those with large investments in conventional photographic equipment who fear that it will become redundant.

One of the great strengths of digital imaging is that almost anyone can learn to do it. The experienced photographer with a lifetime of skills can put them to new and exciting use, while the newcomer can achieve amazing effects from day one. Whatever your level, you'll find that digital technology makes learning new techniques both easy and fun: particularly so because the results are immediate.

As you work through this book, you'll discover various ways of getting images on to your computer. Don't worry if you do not have a digital camera, or even a camera of any sort, you can still enjoy the creative art of digital imaging. You'll start by exploring digital image editing software. Then, with the tools and basics behind you, you'll begin turning good images into great *pictures*.

Image manipulation also makes it easy to create terrific panoramas, or to use cherished photos in a greetings card or calendar. You'll even take a peek at some of the more extreme possibilities offered, like creating unique 3D landscapes, or turning dull, passport-like portraits into bizarre caricatures. And if you want to show off your results, how about creating a website? It's not as difficult as you think.

In *The Digital Photography Workbook* we have turned our backs, as far as possible, on 'techy' jargon. As long as you can use a computer for everyday activities such as word processing, and, ideally, have had some basic encounters with digital imaging software, you'll find you can take the book at a run.

Simon Joinson & Peter Cope, 2002

The tools of digital imaging

Armed with a computer, making your first steps into digital imaging could not be more straightforward. All you need is an image manipulation package (the image editing application) and some digital images.

Although a digital camera is an ideal source of digital photographs, it is not the only one. A desktop scanner is an excellent tool for turning shots from your photo album into digital images. If you've got a 35mm camera or an APS model, then your local photolab can provide a CD filled with digital copies of your shots along with (or instead of) your conventional prints.

When it comes time to produce a real print of your masterpiece, you'll find that even modest inkjet printers are now capable of results that are virtually indistinguishable from 'real' photographic prints. The premature ageing of prints, once the bane of the inkjet, is also increasingly a thing of the past. Treated

If you can have a conventional camera (such as this APS model), you can still get digital images along with your prints at most photolabs.

well, your prints should last at least as long as most conventional prints, and you have the additional reassurance that with digital technology, you can easily make an identical safety copy of your original image file.

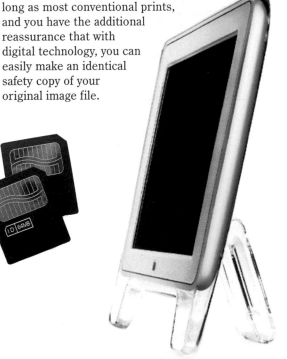

The working environment

If you've never used image editing applications before, a first look can be pretty daunting. Once opened, your screen seems awash with buttons, tools and palettes: you may wonder where to start. So here is a simplified run-down of the main features you'll encounter, and how these are interpreted by different applications. Though there are many more applications than we've shown, those here are typical of the majority.

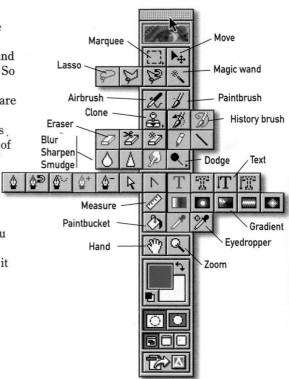

Canvas

Dominating the workspace, the canvas contains the image upon which you are currently working. Using a Zoom tool, you can select whether you see the whole of this image or enlarge a particular area of it for detailed editing. In most applications, two (or more) images can be open simultaneously.

Toolbox

Grouped together in a convenient (and sometimes moveable) block are the tools used to perform edits. These include selection tools (for selecting specific parts of an image), painting tools (such as the Paintbrush and Spraycan, designed to paint on the image), darkroom tools (including tools such as Dodge and Burn that emulate traditional darkroom effects) and other, often specialized tools.

Menus

Whether you choose to work using a Windows application or a Macintosh, you'll find that image editing menus follow the conventional layout for your computer platform. Image editing menus provide access to, for example, effects filters, image layers (sometimes called objects) and additional commands. Through the menus you can also configure advanced settings such as image size, canvas size, colour modes and print options.

Palettes

These are often called floating palettes, because they can be moved around the screen and positioned conveniently. They provide extra control and adjustment for tools and other features. Individual floating palettes might permit the selection of a paintbrush size (or type), or enable image layer management, or colour selection. The range and type of palettes vary from application to application.

Adobe Photoshop

Adobe's Photoshop has become the industry standard by virtue of the comprehensive tools and commands offered along with a working environment that aids effective editing. Though the full application is expensive, junior version Photoshop Elements offers (at a modest price) virtually all the features required by the non-professional digital photographer. Both versions are available for Macintosh and Windows computers.

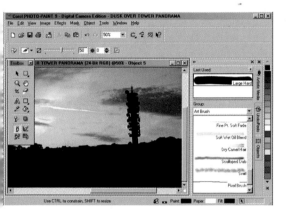

Corel Photo-Paint

Part of the extensive graphics package CorelDRAW!, Photo-Paint is a fully featured image editing package with much the same overall look and functionality as Photoshop. Integration with the vector graphics elements of CorelDRAW! are not seamless, but the two products can be used together to create powerful imagery. Mac and Windows versions are available, along with 'limited' editions such as Photo-Paint Digital Camera Edition (Windows, shown here), that interfaces directly to your digital camera, if you have one.

Jasc Paintshop Pro

This Windows-only application has a working environment similar to that of Photoshop. Many of the palettes are tool-sensitive, displaying pertinent options when a specific tool is selected.

MGI Photosuite

Photosuite is organized somewhat differently to Photoshop. Tools are arranged around the canvas, whilst the controls and information normally found on floating palettes is indicated on the panel to the left.

Getting started

What is a digital image?

There is nothing mysterious about a digital image. Though the term 'digital' has been used – perhaps overused – in worlds as diverse as television, communications and photography, a digital image is no more or less than an image that has been divided into small cells known as pixels. These pixels, or rather the brightness, colour and contrast information that is contained within them, are represented by a digital – that is, numerical – code. It is this numerical code that your computer subsequently manipulates on your command, thereby making it possible for you to edit the image. Of course, you don't actually see the code. Instead, when you use a painting tool you see colour applied; when you adjust a contrast control you get modified contrast.

Using a numerical code to represent an image has other important benefits, too. One of the major such benefits is that you can make identical – truly identical – copies of a code, resulting in identical copies of the image. You can even send that code by e-mail (for example), certain in the knowledge that when it's received at the other end, it can be used to create copies of your images that are 100 percent faithful to the original.

Following are some of the terms that are used to describe digital images, together with their meaning in conventional photographic terms.

Resolution

Unlike its conventional photographic usage, the term 'resolution' when applied to a digital image can describe both the amount of detail in the image and the number of colours present. The first of these factors is described in terms of the number of pixels (the smallest elements of a digital image – see above) that comprise the image. A typical figure might be $1{,}800 \times 1{,}200$ pixels, or, less precisely, 2.1 megapixels, where one megapixel represents one million pixels. Note that it isn't always necesary to use the highest resolution available; web pages, for example, are currently only capable of displaying images at relatively low resolution.

This digital camera image has been reproduced at three resolutions. In the first, two million pixels comprise the image and provide considerable detail. In the next, with 8,500 pixels, the form is still discernible but much of the detail has been lost. In the final example, with less than 500 pixels, very little information remains.

16

The RGB mode is one of two principal colour modes in which colour images are described by the amount of red, green and blue in each pixel. Again, 256 levels are possible for each of the colour components, resulting in the overall possibility of 16 million colours. Images reproduced on a computer monitor (featuring red, green and blue phosphors) are best displayed in this mode.

The second colour mode is CMYK mode. This tends to be used more for images that will ultimately end up in print: the CMYK components (corresponding to the colours cyan, magenta, yellow and black) represent the four ink colours used in colour printing. The range of colours possible in a CMYK image is similar (but not identical) to that in an RGB image.

Greyscale images represent the image using only shades of grey (typically 256 shades in an 8-bit image).

In some later examples you'll discover further, more specialized colour modes.

Bit depth

Bit depth describes the second aspect of the resolution, the number of colours that comprise the image. An image with only black and white tones (and no intermediate greys) is said to have a bit depth of 1. For a sharp photographic image you typically work with a bit depth of 24 (usually described as 24-bit colour). Based on the computer's binary counting system, this yields a palette of over 16 million colours.

Colour mode

Conventional photography recognizes two print types or modes, colour or monochrome. In digital photography, these are subdivided into further categories.

The Greyscale mode delivers images featuring 255 shades of grey, normally from black through to white. These images have an 8-bit depth (since, using the binary system, 2×2×2×2×2×2×2×2 gives 256 possible shades).

A 1-bit image contains only black and white. Increasing the bit depth adds shades of grey and colour. A 24-bit image shows a full range of colours (more than 16 million).

Gathering digital images

Digital cameras

Advances in design and image quality have now made consumer digital cameras a useful and affordable way of gathering digital images. Professional digital cameras – which are still expensive – have for some time supplanted their conventional equivalents in many areas of commercial photography.

Though quality is not specifically dependent on the number of pixels a camera can record, models offering around four megapixels can be used for prints up to A4 size. A3 prints are even possible now with cameras costing less than £1,000.

Most digital cameras have fixed lenses with zoom features (though on cheap models this tends to be the less satisfactory digital zoom). Only the expensive models – often based on conventional SLR designs – offer interchangeable lens mounts.

Picture CD and photo CD

Driven by the need (on the part of photographers and the photographic processing industry) for a practical way of producing digital images from standard film stock, Picture CDs and Photo CDs are now an excellent way to source and store digital images derived from film.

The original Photo CD uses a unique storage method that permits negatives or transparencies to be digitally recorded at

For ultimate quality – at a price – dedicated digital cameras such as this Hasselblad can't be beaten. They produce immediate pictures, a major bonus in commercial photography.

five resolutions, from a 70k file size (suitable for browsing) through to 18MB for high-resolution work. ('Pro' Photo CDs offer a sixth level of resolution – and much higher quality.) PhotoCDs are available from most processing labs from 35mm and APS film (both at the time of processing and later), and can be produced from larger-format films at specialist labs.

Picture CD is similarly a CD-based system, but it offers a *single* resolution with each image taking between 4.5MB and 6MB, depending on film format. Images are saved using the slightly inferior JPEG format (more on the failings of JPEG file format later). Picture CD (strictly a trade name for discs produced by Kodak) and equivalents from other

Cameras such as this Fuji model are extremely compact and can deliver images capable of considerable enlargement. This particular model also permits the recording of low-resolution video clips and even replays MP3 music files.

photolabs are designed essentially for the consumer market, and as such are normally only available at the time of processing. Picture CDs also include free software packages that permit basic image manipulation and image cataloguing.

Scanners

Flatbed – or 'desktop' – scanners provide another way of converting existing images to a digital format. Current models offer very high quality (measured in 'dots per inch' resolution) and good colour fidelity. When buying one, check the optical resolution: this should be at least 600×600 dots per inch. Don't be seduced by higher figures quoted as 'interpolated' resolution. These figures – often much higher – are created in the scanner's software, and do not reflect any greater detail in the image.

Slide scanners

If you have an extensive collection of slides or negatives, a slide scanner is an ideal way of digitizing your images. Slide scanners act on the same principal as flatbed scanners, but offer a much higher resolution. Most models accept 35mm media and – normally with an adapter – APS cartridges. More expensive models can also accept medium-format slides and negatives. Usefully, the software provided with many models can remove (during the scanning process) scratches and blemishes on the film, saving much time later.

Ready-made images

Distributed via the Internet or on CD, there is a host of ready-made images available for your use. Many are free, some require payment (often according to intended use), and some have restrictions on use (for example, they may be used freely for personal projects but not for commercial purposes). You'll need to check the terms and conditions of each image before using it. Note, too, that most image editing applications feature sample images for you to experiment with.

SLR digital cameras cost more than equivalents using film, but are becoming increasingly common.

Photo CDs and Picture CDs provide an easy method of using digital images on your computer.

Reducing your workload

Although it may seem that anything is possible in the digital darkroom, it makes sense for you to get your images as good as possible before resorting to digital techniques: that way you'll save time that can then be used creatively at the computer. Here are a few tricks to ensure you start work with the best-quality digital images.

Getting the best from a digital camera

White balance

Unlike film-based cameras that need filmstock appropriate to the lighting source, digital cameras can be set to the characteristics of virtually any light source. This feature is known as the white balance. You can set the white balance on most models to daylight (full sun or overcast) and a range of specific artificial lighting types. In this way, unwanted colour casts in your image are fixed. You can also set the white balance control to 'auto', which is particularly useful when working in mixed lighting conditions. Digital cameras are particularly adept at handling fluorescent lighting, a problem area for conventional film.

Digital zoom

Some basic digital cameras – and quite a few midrange models – feature a digital zoom, either in place of, or in addition to a conventional optical zoom. It works by expanding and recording only the central part of the image, and in doing so, records the image at much lower resolution. There is absolutely no benefit in this. Record your scene without the digital zoom and you can achieve the same effect using software later; and with a 'full' image, you could alter the crop afterwards for better results.

In-camera special effects

Some cameras (usually basic to midrange models) allow you to apply special effects (such as sepia toning, posterisation, star

Use the white balance control to remove unwanted colour casts – or to set a cast where this is required for creative effect. Here, a tungsten light source is recorded with the white balance set to daylight (left) and tungsten (right).

In-camera effects may look good at the time, but they make future edits of the original image difficult. Here the original image has been sepia-toned using the camera's 'Sepia' effect.

Image enlargement

Similarly, there is no gain in scanning at a higher resolution, even if you intend to print the scanned image at a higher resolution. You can change the image's size and characteristics more effectively later.

Magazine, fine art and newspaper images

If you want to scan an image from one of these sources, there's a strong possibility that the dot pattern that comprises the image will interfere with the scanning pattern of the scanner head, resulting in what are known as *moiré* fringes. You can prevent this by setting the Descreen control in the scanner software to the appropriate setting for the source image.

filter effects and more) to a recorded image. Beware. It's always best to record the image without such effects. With digital imaging software you can apply your choice of thousands of such effects to your image once you have captured it, whereas an in-camera effect cannot be removed.

Image storage

Contemporary cameras create largish image files – perhaps 12MB or so. To get a reasonable number on to the camera's memory card requires each file to be compressed. Such compression can be mild or extreme, the latter producing an image that is subsequently lower in quality. Where quality is important, ensure that you record images at the best quality possible: this is normally described as 'best' or 'fine' quality. The drawback, of course, is that you'll be able to store far fewer images when the file size is large.

Effective scanning

If you are using a scanner to digitize your images, here are a few tips for getting the best results.

Understanding image resolution

If you are scanning a photograph (even a high-quality print made on pin-sharp material such as Ilfochrome), the equivalent resolution will be no more than 233 dots per inch. So there is little point in scanning at a significantly higher resolution: 300dpi should be sufficient.

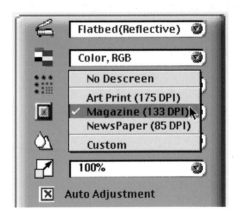

This scanner software will prevent *moiré* effects when the appropriate source media is selected.

Bit depth

Many scanners can be set to scan at different bit depths, with consequential effect on the image size. Normally, 24-bit colour is sufficient. Scanning at 36- or even 48-bit will result in an image that features far more subtle gradations, but it will almost always need to be converted to 24-bit colour for further processing and printing.

Your computer as digital darkroom

Hardware considerations

Such is the power of contemporary computers that most are suitable for image editing duties, virtually straight out of the box.

Clock speed

Computer manufacturers boast about the overall clock speed of their wares – that is, the speed at which the central processing chip can handle instructions. But this is only partially relevant. You may have the fastest processor available, but if the speed of the components that deliver and take away information from the processor is slow, you'll have a log jam.

If you are in the market for a new computer, ask for benchmark timings. These give a more accurate indication of overall performance than do processor speeds. If you can, ask for benchmarks that relate to image editing or graphics applications, which use the processor in a different way to applications such as office software.

Finally, it's worth bearing in mind that not all processor clock speeds are equivalent. Typical Macintosh processors – PowerPCs – offer performance similar to PC processors with twice the clock speed.

Memory

Computer experts will always say that you can never have too much memory, and for digital imaging this is absolutely correct. Digital image files are large – and manipulating them demands plenty of memory headroom. Though 128MB of RAM – random access memory – is commonplace today, the demands of your operating system and other concurrent processes can be such that most of this is consumed in everyday operation, leaving little for your image editor. Consider adding at least another 128MB. Then you can be reasonably sure of swift performance. And don't be seduced into thinking that virtual memory – a sort of 'simulated RAM' using the hard disc – is a substitute. It is just too slow.

Monitors

Computer monitors, by and large, are pretty good in terms of their colour reproduction.

Led by Apple's range of Studio and Cinema displays, LCD panels are now credible for image editing work.

Adding more RAM is one of the best ways to improve the performance of your computer – go for as much as you can afford.

The calibration routine supplied with Adobe's Photoshop ensures that the image you see on the screen prints out almost identically.

You can calibrate them to be even better, by using software supplied with your image editing application, or perhaps even by the hardware manufacturer. Proper calibration ensures that the image seen on screen will be accurately reproduced on a printer of equivalent accuracy.

LCD displays, once inferior to conventional cathode ray tube monitors, are now suitable for exacting work too.

Peripherals

Whilst some peripherals – scanners and slide scanners for example – are desirable, others are essential. In this category come removable disc drives and, for most users, printers.

Digital images tend to produce large files, and collections of these can soon fill your computer's hard disc. Copying these to, say, a Zip® drive or a recordable CD makes sense, for two reasons. First, it frees space on your hard disc. Second, by making multiple backup copies you can keep your image collection safe from hard disc problems, which are all too frequent.

Mac vs PC

There is a constant debate about which is best for image editing – a Macintosh or a Windows-based PC. In practice the question is largely irrelevant: you'll be governed by the computer you have, or by the system you prefer.

It is fair to say that the Macintosh, by virtue of its hardware and software architecture, has the edge in running graphics-based applications: but the differences are mostly slight. If you are adept at exploiting Windows and have a Windows PC, you need not feel unduly compromised. Just as important is to enhance the performance of either platform by addressing the issues we've highlighted here.

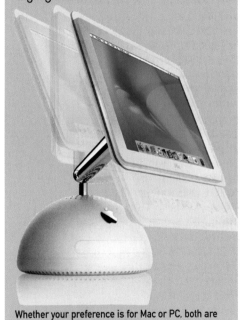

Whether your preference is for Mac or PC, both are capable of excellent image editing.

Whatever media you use, it is essential to back up regularly.

Understanding file formats

Digital images can be saved in any of a number of file formats. They are all equally valid, but your intended use of the image has a significant bearing on which you should adopt.

Compression: JPEGs and TIFFs

The first concept to understand is compression. Files have to be compressed in order to fit a suitable number of images on to a camera's memory card. Or, you might need to compress the image files on your computer in order to e-mail them to a friend.

When files are compressed, you can use a 'lossy' method, in which detail is irretrievably removed in order to make the file size smaller; or you can use a 'lossless' method, in which all data is preserved. Lossy methods can deliver very small files: the most common example of this technique is the JPEG (standing for Joint Photographic Experts Group), with the file extension .JPG. Many digital cameras use the JPEG format, which is also employed by Kodak in their Picture CD system. Using modest compression, very little data (i.e. image detail) is lost, but the effect can be cumulative. If you repeatedly open and save an image in JPEG format, the degradation will increase.

The TIFF format uses a compression regime called LZW (Lempel-Ziv-Welch, after its creators) that results in no data being lost. At the risk of being simplistic, you can describe this method as squeezing the data up more tightly rather than throwing some of it away, as is the case with JPEG. A file compressed in the TIFF format is generally larger than a corresponding JPEG file.

Most image editors have their own format – often called the native format – that preserves the information (such as image layers and other characteristics) that the particular application supports. Photoshop, for example, uses the .PSD format for its native files.

When you are using a digital camera, file compression becomes particularly important. Without it, your camera's memory card would very quickly fill up;

More file formats

PICT

A high-quality, 'lossless' compression regime normally only suitable for use on and with Macintosh computers.

GIF

A family of formats (that include GIF89a and Transparent GIF) that can display up to 256 colours. Though widely used on the web, the restricted colour palette limits their use elsewhere.

EPS

Encapsulated PostScript, a format used for vector graphics (rather than the bitmap graphics of images).

BMP

Used mainly by Windows computers to save monochrome or colour images at colour depths up to 24-bit.

PCX

Largely superseded, this format was originally used for the DOS program PC Paintbrush.

An image saved using the JPEG format (below left) shows considerable loss of detail compared with the same image stored using the lossless TIFF format (right).

even a large, 128MB memory card holds only a handful of the 17MB image files created by many digital cameras in uncompressed form. However, not all images need to be stored at high resolution, so a range of compressions is offered. This gives users the opportunity to select a compression to meet their needs. Important images, for example, could be stored at high resolution, and more casual shots at a lower one; in this way you can optimize the quality and number of images gathered before you download them to your computer.

Mastering image editing basics

Getting familiar with editing tools

L et's start by exploring the tools and commands offered by image editors. Here, they are broken into logical groups to make their actions and effects easier to understand.

Painting tools

Painting tools have one purpose: to lay 'paint' on the image canvas, overlaying the colours already there.

Paintbrushes paint with a selected colour. Using a setting in the corresponding palette, the size (and sometimes the shape) of the paintbrush can be adjusted. A similar Pencil tool produces a fine, hard-edged line. A softer effect is achieved with the Airbrush tool that mimics the actions of an artist's airbrush.

By painting with adjacent pixels (rather than a solid paint colour), the Clone tool can obliterate intrusive elements. Conversely, it can add new features to an otherwise bland landscape.

The Clone tool (called Rubber Stamp in Photoshop) is a unique and very powerful painting tool. Rather than painting with a colour, it paints with parts of an image. If you want to hide a feature (such as street furniture or unwanted people), the clone tool is ideal.

The Paintbrush, Airbrush and Pencil tools (top, middle and bottom left) provide different methods of laying colour on the canvas.

Selection tools

It is easy, when using any of the painting tools, to paint beyond the intended area. Using one of the selection tools, you can select only part of an image and make that receptive to the paint (or, indeed, any transformation or manipulation). Again, image manipulation software provides you with several options for selecting particular image elements.

Marquee tools are the simplest, both in use and in the features offered. They allow

The Marquee tool is ideal for framing (and cropping) an image, or, as here, creating a vignette.

Where the subject has a consistent colour, the Magic Wand is an ideal tool.

Providing the subject has a definite 'edge,' the Magnetic Lasso is one of the easiest tools for making a selection.

rectangular or oval shapes to be selected. Working freehand, you simply draw from a start point (or corner) to an end point. The tool takes no account of the image itself. A marquee might be used when cropping an image, or to create a vignette effect.

The Lasso tool permits a freehand selection of an object *in* the image. The lasso is drawn around the perimeter of the object to be selected, and once the selection is 'closed', the enclosed area becomes active, ready for manipulation.

27

The Sponge is an excellent way to enhance elements of an image by increasing (or decreasing) the colour saturation.

Manipulation tools

It should not come as too much of a surprise to find that some of the conventional darkroom stalwarts have equivalents in digital imaging.

Dodge and Burn tools are exactly analogous to their darkroom counterparts. They can selectively burn in (increase density; darken) or dodge (reduce image intensity; lighten). As with brush tools, you can select a tool shape then control the intensity with which the effect is applied.

The Sponge tool has no conventional darkroom equivalent. You can use it selectively to increase (or decrease) the colour saturation within an image.

Arguably the most often used – and misused – tools are Sharpen and Blur. An often-quoted benefit of image editing software is the ability to sharpen blurred photos. Actually, no digital technique can restore detail to an image that was not there in the first place. However, it is possible to increase the *perceived*

Variations on the Lasso include the Polygonal Lasso, that draws straight-sided shapes, and the Magnetic Lasso. The latter, detecting the edge of your subject, automates the selection process by then following it, although the results are not always perfect.

The Magic Wand tool selects on the basis of colour rather than shape. By clicking with the wand in an area of continuous colour, all adjacent pixels will be selected. A Tolerance control can be adjusted to add more or less similarly coloured pixels to the selection and this in turn makes the selection more precise.

Masks provide another method of selection. When you apply a Mask to an image, you apply a 'protective coating' to those parts that you do not want changed. More of this later.

The Sharpen tool is not a cure for poor focusing, but a method of improving sharpness. Overuse, however can seriously degrade image quality.

sharpness in an image. The Sharpen tool works by identifying changes of contrast in the image and making the transition across this boundary narrower.

The Sharpen tool should be applied with care: overuse, or extreme use, can introduce unpleasant (and very obvious) image artefacts, as shown here (left).

Blur tools have the opposite effect: they reduce image sharpness. You might use this technique, for example, to emphasize your subject by softening its surroundings. Some blur tools permit blurring to be applied in a very specialized way. The Radial Blur, for example, produces a rotational blur around a pre-determined point: it could be used on a car wheel, say, to imply movement. Zoom blur introduces a blurring effect away from a point, simulating the effect of operating the camera's zoom lens during a long exposure.

Not only but also ...

Many of the principal tools have been covered here, but we have still only scratched the surface. The step-by-step projects that form the main sections of this book illustrate the potential of image editing software in far greater depth.

Zoom Blur is a controllable way of introducing zoom lens effects to your image.

Filters and effects

Coloured Pencil

Diffuse Glow

Filters, sometimes called Effects, are powerful features of image editing applications. Originally conceived as the digital equivalents of photographic filters, there are now countless thousands available. No longer restricted to simulating photographic filters, they can now be used to convert images into 'watercolours,' 'mosaics' or even, should you be so inclined, neon fantasies.

Some filters are blatant and produce images so stylized that they can be justified only on occasion, for very specific uses. Others, such as those that introduce grain or mistiness, can – and will – be used more widely. Sharpen and Blur filters perform the same function as the toolbar tools we've previously discussed, but in many cases they provide more control over the extent of application.

Look out for third-party filters, too. Often called plug-in filters, these can be added to your image editor's plug-in folder, and will seamlessly integrate with the host application (check compatibility with your application before installing).

Ocean Ripple

Plastic Wrap

Find Edges

Tiles

The Filter effects used here are typical of those offered with image editing applications. They provide an easy way to liven up an image but should be used with purpose: overuse (and misuse) can lead to unpleasant results.

Lens Flare

Watercolour

Layers and objects

Complex image editing can be made simpler by working with image *layers* – called Objects in some applications (such as Photo-Paint). A layered image is built up rather in the manner that a cartoon animator builds his scenes. First comes the background image (normally the original image, prior to any changes). Above this are transparent layers – rather like the acetate cells of the animator – upon which image manipulations are applied or artwork is painted.

The clear benefit of a layered image is that it gives you the ability to edit layers – or the background – selectively. You can even change the order of the layers in the 'stack' or remove them entirely, so, if you decide that edits performed on the image are inappropriate or need further modification, you can do so working only on one layer, rather than compromising the whole image.

You can either save an image with the layer information preserved, or if no further editing is planned, a layered image can be 'flattened' into the background.

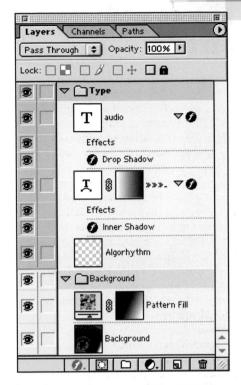

Image layers can be monitored (and manipulated) using the Layers Palette (such as the Photoshop example shown here). Layers can be moved relative to each other, deleted or copied.

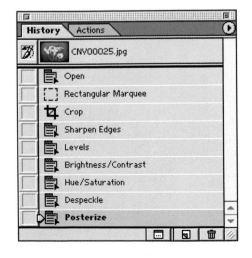

History

Another useful feature for non-destructive editing is History. Not available in all image editors, History permits your image editing steps to be retraced, and, where necessary, individual steps to be removed. This is useful when you realize – sometime after the event – that you have made (say) an incorrect adjustment or applied the wrong filter.

The steps used to create this posterized image are given in the History palette. You can remove individual steps by pulling the appropriate line to the wastebasket.

The good, the bad and the ugly

This overview has so far looked specifically at those features common to most image editing applications. Though they vary in detail from one application to another, operationally they are very similar.

There are also some unique tools that either offer quick solutions, or are just downright wacky. Here are three examples:

Colour variations

Photoshop's Variations command is an easy way to assess and adjust the colour balance of an image. Rather than attempt to make subjective assessments, Variations provides comparison views of the same image with slightly different colour biases. You can also make similar assessments of the brightness of your image.

Painting with pictures

The Picture Tube feature of Paintshop Pro lets you paint with images and graphics. Either using one of the supplied image sets (that include coins, pool balls, cars and insects, as shown here), or your own image elements, you can paint across your image. You'll probably find this tool is better suited to creating graphic images than to manipulating photographs but as with many editing tools, a little inspiration can produce excellent results.

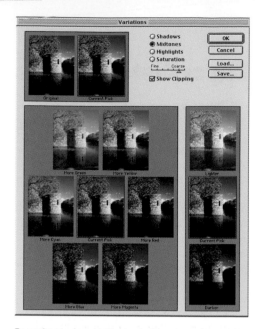

Removing a colour cast is simple if you can compare different colour bias versions of the same image.

Warped

In several applications you can find tools with names such as Mesh Warp and Liquefy, which permit freeform distortion of images. Use them for comic effect (distorting facial features, or changing the physical characteristics of pets), or for inflating/ deflating, pushing and prodding the canvas into subtly or grossly distorted forms.

The Picture Tube will not be used by Paintshop Pro experts on a daily basis, but it does offer some interesting graphics opportunities.

Whether used to improve on nature or to create bizarre landscapes, the Mesh Warp tool offers intriguing possibilities.

Specialist software

Not all image editors are designed to undertake a wide range of editing jobs. Some have a more specific purpose. There are both self-contained applications dedicated to a particular process, and others that provide tools to produce specialized images for subsequent editing in a conventional image editor. Many of these are high-end, professional products, but a few have found their way into the consumer marketplace, including the following:

A wider view

Photovista is the leading exponent of a software class that has just one purpose: to convert a series of consecutive images into a single, seamless panorama. This may seem a somewhat limited application (there is only so much you can do with a panoramic shot), but it is useful for creating ultra-wide views, overcoming some of the wide-angle limitations of digital cameras. There is also an increasing requirement (particularly on the web) for 'immersive' views, and this application is ideal for the purpose.

Though Photoshop Elements and Photosuite 4 offer panorama-creating tools, Photovista is still the most effective, and offers the greatest range of control.

Having fun

Some applications defy categorization and have no serious purpose. SuperGoo is the most prominent example. It turns photos of faces into caricatures or can be used to add 'furniture' such as earrings, beards, glasses or even new facial features. For good measure (and practice), there is a gallery of faces included within the software.

It does just one thing, but does it very well. Supergoo is definitely a 'fun' application.

Visiting new worlds

Though not an image editing application, Corel's Bryce is a useful adjunct. With it, you can create new landscapes, skyscapes (and more) to add to (or replace) scenes in your existing images. It has an easy-to-use interface and – be warned – can become quite addictive.

With Photovista you can take a number of individual shots and automatically combine them into a seamless panorama.

The completed panorama is successfully joined, even when the source images were, as in this case, taken with a wide angle lens.

Simple photo correction and retouching

Adjusting exposure

Modern cameras are pretty good at getting the exposure right most of the time. Matrix and multi-zone metering systems can deliver great results in the most adverse conditions, but there will always be the odd occasion when either the camera gets it wrong, or you might prefer a lighter (or darker) result. Digital cameras also have a tendency to produce rather flat, grey results that can be quickly revitalized using a simple technique.

The image below is typical of beach scenes where reflected light from the sand and sky have caused underexposure.

Though not fully underexposed, it is slightly underexposed, and lacks the *punch* of the original scene, with flat colour.

Correcting – or adjusting – the exposure is simple. And because corrections such as this tend to be used extensively, you'll find many image editors feature commands designed to fix this specific problem.

Applying the Auto Enhance feature produces a brighter print with extra colour saturation: just what you want.

In this case, Auto Enhance has delivered a good result. This won't always happen, but there is an alternative – the same result can be achieved with 'manual' controls – read on ...

Reflected light from the sand and sky have caused underexposure *(above)*. This has been fully corrected using Auto Enhance *(left)*.

Brightness

The brightness control lets you adjust the overall brightness of the image from (virtually) black through to totally washed out. With more modest settings, you can brighten an underexposed image or hold back (or dim) an overexposed one.

Using Brightness to enhance an image.

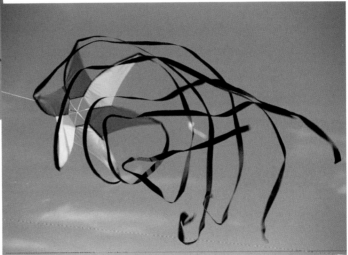

Contrast

Using the contrast control lets you alter the distribution of tones within the image. Sliding the contrast control to the right increases the contrast, making brighter-than-average parts of the image even brighter, and darker parts even darker. Overall brightness and colour saturation is unaffected.

The contrast control is ideal for livening up 'flat' images or, conversely, for subduing garish colours.

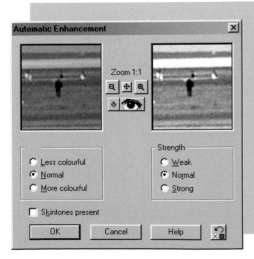

The quick fix

Image editors tend to have different ways of implementing quick-fix commands. In Photoshop, as befits this professional-level product, you can use the Auto Levels command. This automatically adjusts the spread and distribution of tonal levels within the image to deliver a better result.

In many other applications you'll find features such as Auto Enhance that work by altering the brightness, contrast and saturation of the image so that it reflects an average value for the image.

Saturation

Sometimes called the Colour control, the Saturation control adjusts the strength of the colours in the image, but does not affect the tones (blacks, whites and greys). At its minimum setting (with the saturation at zero) you get a greyscale image. At full saturation, colours in the image become fully saturated and (for most purposes) too bright and garish.

The perfect combination

It's unlikely that any one of the controls just described will deliver an improved image on its own. You'll need to manipulate all three. Ultimately, you'll find that you can achieve more effective (as well as more controlled) results using these manual features in preference to any Auto Enhance control.

The Saturation control can bring about profound changes in the colour of an image.

The Marquee: selecting, cutting and feathering

The Marquee is the simplest and, in some ways, the most obvious of selection tools. Unlike all other selection tools, it is 'subject independent', meaning that whereas tools such as the Lasso and Magic Wand are designed to follow the contours of an object within the image, the Marquee makes a selection based on a geometric form within the image frame.

Though some applications permit a range of shapes (such as stars or polygons), the universal implementation of the Marquee uses rectangular or oval shapes.

To make a selection, first select the Marquee tool, then click the mouse at the intended start position (typically the top left hand corner). Next, you drag the mouse to the opposite corner (in the case of the oval Marquee, the oval will be drawn within this box).

If you wish to draw a square or circle, there is often a *modifier* key – a key that is pressed while dragging the mouse. In the case of Photoshop, the modifier is the shift key.

Using the Marquee

Bearing in mind that the Marquee does not make a selection on the basis of the contents of an image, on what occasions does it come into its own? A principal use is to *crop* images. Though there are dedicated crop tools, the Marquee can also be used to define the part of the image to be *retained*.

If you wanted to trim this image to retain only the central rose, you would drag the Marquee across the area you wished to save. The Marquee is marked by a dotted line, often referred to as 'marching ants' on account of its animated appearance. Selecting the Crop command from the menu (or pressing a Crop button) removes the area outside your selection. It is important to note that the cropped image will be proportionately smaller than the original.

Using the Marquee to add print borders

You can use a similar procedure to the one just described to create borders around prints. This time, rather than cropping to the Marquee boundary, you will *remove* the surroundings of the image but maintain the original image dimensions. Here's how.

1 Draw the Marquee over your image to leave a slim, regular border all round.

2 Invert the image selection. This makes the border active, rather than the area within the Marquee. The Invert selection command is usually found in the Select menu.

3 Choose a colour for your border. Make this your background colour. For clarity, white has been chosen here: this is the normal default background colour in most image editors.

4 Press delete. The image in the border area will disappear to be replaced with the border colour.

For a more sophisticated effect, you could add a black keyline around the image between the print area and the border.

1 Create a border as above, but choose black as the background colour.

5 Repeat the process, drawing a border around the image and a fine piece of the black border. Change the background colour to white and press delete.

Feathered selections

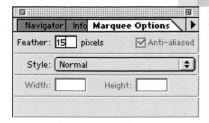

The Marquee selections made so far have been *hard edged*: when cropping and creating borders, the image was trimmed precisely at the point of the Marquee. There will be times when you don't want such a hard edge. On such occasions you can use the Feather command to make your selection – with the Marquee or other tools – soft edged.

When you use Feathering you will be asked to specify a Feather radius: this is the distance (in image pixels) over which you want the transition to occur, from solid image to transparent. This can be entered in the appropriate dialogue box or options palette for the tool. Here, a radius of 15 pixels has been set.

In the following images, increasing Feather radii have been applied. Note that the image fade occurs either side of the boundary determined by the Marquee.

Feathering a selection becomes increasingly important – and useful – when you start creating image *montages*. Montages comprise images composed of elements from several different source images; giving a soft boundary to potentially disparate elements helps create a natural blend and avoids the 'paper collage' effect when hard-edged selections are used.

Feather Radius 10 pixels.

Feather Radius 20 pixels.

Feather Radius 40 pixels.

Feather Radius 30 pixels.

Creating a vignette

A creative and attractive application of the Marquee tool – which also uses the Feather command – is to create a vignette image. These were popular in Victorian and Edwardian days, when they were used to display portraits and views. Here, the same image is given three different treatments.

In the final treatment, a sepia tone was applied to create the feel of a Victorian print. This was achieved by Colourizing the image to give the tone, then increasing the lightness of the image (and border) to give the aged, faded look.

In some image editing applications, sepia filters can achieve the same effect. In others (for example, Photoshop), select Image menu▸Adjust▸Hue/Saturation, choose the Colorize button and adjust hue until the desired colour is achieved.

1 Choose your image, making sure that there is adequate space around the main subject and little of importance in the corners. This picture-postcard of an English castle is ideal.

2 Select the Oval (Elliptical) Marquee tool and drag it across the image. Set the Feather radius to (say) 30 pixels (the best setting will depend upon the size and resolution of your image: you may need to make adjustments to get the optimum result).

3 Invert the selection and delete the border.

For this alternative version the background has been
converted to black, simulating the presentation of the image
on black board, above; or to sepia, below.

Vignette tips

A circular vignette can be effective, but combined with a black
border it can have the unfortunate effect of making the result look like
a telescopic view.

For antique or traditional effects, print your vignette on to textured
paper.

If you tint your images, don't restrict the colour to sepia. A deep
indigo tint can simulate selenium toning, and don't forget that more
vibrant colours, such as reds and greens, can suit certain subjects.

Lassoing: making selections based on shape

In the simple example here, the Freehand Lasso is ideal for describing the edge of this bloom.

The Marquee tool is ideal for frames and vignettes, where the selections are based on rectangles and ellipses, (*see* pages 38–41), but it is completely unsuitable for making selections of irregular objects within an image. Fortunately, there is an alternative – the Lasso tool. With the Lasso, you can describe the boundaries of an object and have everything within that boundary selected.

In fact, the Lasso tool is a family of tools. Though the family varies in size according to the image editing application in use, there are three basic variations.

Use the Freehand Lasso to select an object by drawing – freehand – around its boundaries.

Use the Magnetic Lasso to draw a selection automatically. This intelligent tool identifies the edge of the selection and attaches itself neatly. It isn't foolproof – it can go astray where contrast is low or there are alternate edges – but it is great for making complex selections.

The Polygonal Lasso can be used to describe multi-sided selections using straight line segments. It is especially useful for selecting buildings and architectural details.

Using each of the Lasso types is easy.

On closer inspection, however, you can see that the boundary has not been precisely defined.

The freehand Lasso is best reserved for making rough selections when testing out an effect, for example, or for situations where pinpoint accuracy is not required. An example of the latter might be a feathered selection or vignette where an informal, freehand shape was required rather than something more geometric.

You could achieve a more precise effect by working more slowly, or by enlarging the image further. But why create additional work for yourself when you can use the Magnetic Lasso?

Freehand Lasso

1 Select the tool.

2 With the mouse button pressed, drag the cursor around the area you wish to select.

3 Release the mouse button when you are at, or very close to the start point.

Tips

The Add To Selection feature enables an imprecise selection to be refined by adding to it any parts that were not selected. Normally, any selection tool can be used to add elements to a selection, not just the tool used to make the original selection.

The Polygonal Lasso can also be used to select curved shapes. Simply click at short intervals around the perimeter.

Magnetic Lasso

1 The Magnetic Lasso is used in a slightly different way. Click with the mouse on the start point of the selection, then release the mouse button.

2 Draw around the selection with the mouse button released. Fastening points appear periodically around the edges of the selection.

3 You can add extra fastening points by clicking with the mouse (useful if the selection line wanders from your chosen path).

4 Close the selection by dragging over the start point.

Here is the same selection as the one previously shown, made this time with the Magnetic Lasso. Note how the boundary has been followed more closely, although at a few points (where the boundary is less distinct) there are still some incorrect selections. You will need to attend to these later (using, for example, the Add To Selection feature).

Polygonal Lasso

1 Click the mouse to determine the first, fixed point (usually a corner).

2 Move the mouse to the next corner and click again. A straight line will be drawn between the two points.

3 Continue with additional edges, finally clicking again at the start point.

Architectural subjects such as the church above are ideal for the Polygonal Lasso. Small details can be included by drawing short sides.

There is no practical limit to the number of sides that your polygon can have; when you are tracing a complex shape (such as some of the architectural detail in this example) you can click repeatedly at every corner. Do take care, however, not to be too fast. If you click on two points in very quick succession, the computer will interpret that as the instruction to 'close' the selection. The result will be a selection based on the points drawn so far, joined back to the start point – not what you had intended.

Exploring colour modes

A major part of digital image manipulation involves combining images. To do this effectively, you need to explore the concepts of colour modes and resolution.

Using two (or more) images together requires a little more preparation, and, in particular, needs both images to be compatible. In this context 'compatible' means that both images should be of similar resolution – that is, that the pixel dimensions of each are either similar or can be made similar – and that each image is of the same image mode. In conventional photography you have two principal image modes: black and white, and colour. In digital photography, you have more. Here's a summary of the principal modes and their uses.

The digital equivalent of conventional black and white is the Greyscale mode. Greyscale images (see below) contain all shades of grey, along with black and white.

In Bitmap mode, the image is reduced to (just) black and white tones. When a greyscale image is converted to bitmap,

This greyscale image (above) has been converted to Bitmap mode (below).

greys lighten, median values become white, and those darker become black.

The Duotone mode is somewhat anomalous – a monochrome image to which an additional colour has been added. This can produce potent images when used effectively, though it tends to be used mostly in the printing world to introduce a little colour into otherwise monochrome images. Tritone and Quadtone modes are similar, but with two and three added colours respectively.

RGB (red, green, blue) mode is a popular full-colour mode, used to represent colour images on computer monitors. CMYK (cyan, magenta, yellow, black) mode is a similar full-colour mode that is used for images intended for print (cyan, magenta, yellow and black are the colours of the inks used in colour printing). There are minor differences (due to the practical methods of representation) between CMYK and RGB colour modes.

You might, exceptionally, encounter alternate colour modes such as Lab Color or Indexed Color. These tend to have specialized uses. Virtually all the examples in this book were created in RGB mode prior to conversion to CMYK at the printing stage.

Green has been introduced to a black and white image to create this duotone. See also page 73.

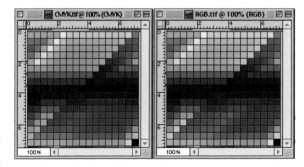

The same image in RGB and CMYK mode. Differences are very slight and subtle.

Image modes tip

Experimenting with image modes can cause irreversible changes to your treasured photos. Make a copy of the image first, then perform the changes. When you convert an image to greyscale, the colour information is discarded and can't normally be retrieved.

Resolution

Image editors display images as bitmaps – in other words, as grids of square pixels. When you want to add one image element to another, image pixels of one image will overlay those of the background. If the two images are not to the same scale (i.e. if the resolutions are not the same), they will not blend as intended.

Fortunately, you can rescale images to get over this problem. Here are examples of two dialogue boxes that appear when an image is rescaled – permitting both physical as well as pixel size changes.

Use either of these dialogue boxes to specify the size that an image will be when printed or displayed on a computer screen (via a website, for example). If the image is to be printed using a desktop inkjet printer,

Tip

Don't change sizes too many times using the same image or image element. Each time an image is resized, pixels will be interpolated (that is, pixels are created based on the average colour values of adjacent pixels) to create the image at the new scale.

When pixels are created in this manner (whether the process involves new ones being added or the total number being reduced), there is a detrimental effect on the sharpness and absolute resolution of the image: such images tend to lose critical sharpness. Though techniques exist to increase the perceived sharpness again, these cannot actually restore the information that has been lost.

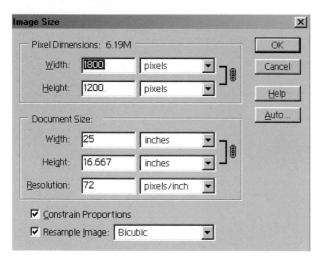

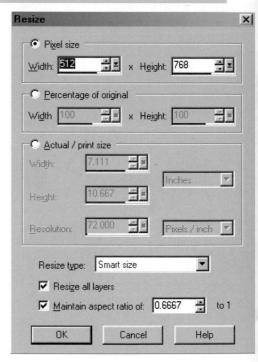

a resolution of 300 pixels per inch is usually sufficient. For screen images (which are limited by the resolution of the computer monitor), 72 pixels per inch is the conventional setting.

Such dialogues normally maintain the proportions (the ratio of height to width) of your image; change the width, and the new height will automatically be set. If you need to change the proportions (say to fit a photo frame aperture or a space on a web page), click on the Constrain Proportions button or Maintain Aspect Ratio (depending on the dialogue).

Now for a creative application of image combination – see page 44: the use of one image to provide a border for another one. (There is no reason always to use plain colours for image borders.)

The idea of framing an image is to set off the subject to its best advantage: a frame should never compete for attention with the image. If your frame is too distracting, blur your framing image or, perhaps, mute the colours slightly.

For a different effect, use the original image, enlarged, as your frame. Blurring the image (or otherwise altering it) is now even more important to ensure differentiation.

1 Start with the original image. Perform any image edits on this that you wish to.

2 Open the second image, without closing the first. This will be your frame. Resize this such that it is (say) 30 per cent larger in both width and height. This will give you a 15 per cent border all around. Ensure that the image has the same resolution as the original.

3 Switch back to the original image and select the entire image. Choose Edit>Copy to copy this image to the clipboard.

4 Paste the copied image into the second image and position centrally.

5 Blurring has been applied to the frame to separate the images.

Two versions of the same image. In the right-hand image the border has been desaturated to remove the colour.

Making selections using colour

T hough the Marquee is an effective selection tool, it is designed for selecting geometric shapes rather than elements from within the

In this image, you want to select only the green plastic. Though it is made of single-coloured plastic, the effects of light and shade introduce a surprising range of colours.

image. For most image editing and image manipulation purposes, you need to select areas – or objects – within the image, whether to copy them or, perhaps, enhance them.

The Magic Wand tool is designed to help you make

When you use the Magic Wand with a setting of 0 for the Tolerance, very little is selected.

Increasing the tolerance to 10 allows a greater selection.

Magic Wand tips

Try to avoid setting the Tolerance too high: otherwise you risk selecting unwanted areas of the image (as here, where a plume of sky has been attached).

Use multiple applications (with a modest Tolerance) to add to the selection, in preference to a larger tolerance setting.

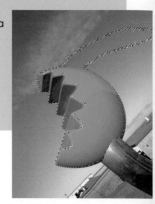

selections based on the colour properties of the intended selection – in the example here, the object colour.

When you select an area of colour with the tip of the Magic Wand tool, all adjacent pixels with the same colour values are added to the selection. How many are selected will depend upon the colour range that you allow for the tool – that is, how far the pixels can vary from the selected colour. This is known as Colour Range or Tolerance (depending on the application), and can be set by the user to help refine the selection.

Incorporating any remaining points can be done by increasing the Tolerance further, or (as most image editors allow) by adding to the selection by repeated applications of the magic wand.

It isn't until the Tolerance is increased to 50 that all the green (save a few white highlights) is selected.

Increasing it to 30, even more so.

Using the Magic Wand to replace a sky

Why not ...

... build up a library of skies for use in pepping up shots? Take skyscapes at different times of the day and in different directions. You can then be sure of having the ideal sky to paste into your scene.

Suppose you have a plain blue sky and want to replace it with a more dramatic one. You might even want to create your own skyscape and use it to replace the one that's currently there. If you want to do either of these things, the Magic Wand is an excellent tool for selecting the sky.

Here's a case in point. The aim is to replace the rather plain blue sky in the image above with a more cloud-laden one.

Tips

When pasting from one scene to another, ensure that your images correspond in scale.

Make new skies realistic by maintaining perspective. In the example on this page the 'new' sky appears to be in the same relationship to the horizon as the one it is replacing.

1 Use the Magic Wand tool to select the sky. Here a modest Tolerance of 20 is used, and added successively to the selection until the whole contiguous sky is selected.

2 Add any remaining areas such as the clouds near the horizon, again using the Magic Wand, until the whole sky area becomes a single selection.

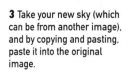

3 Take your new sky (which can be from another image), and by copying and pasting, paste it into the original image.

4 The result is a much more dramatic scene.

49

Changing the colour of a textured subject

Altering the colour of an object is easy when that object has a solid (or even graduated) colour. But if the tone and hues vary over the surface, you need to be more cunning.

1 Begin by selecting the car's paint-work. This is a good case for using the Magic Wand tool, with a modest Tolerance setting.

2 As the paintwork has pronounced boundaries, you might have used the Lasso (page 42) – in such situations the Magnetic Lasso can be particularly effective. But with this particular image, the Lasso would not have been ideal. The headlamps, glass and even the indicators would have been within the main selection boundaries and would have had to be removed – a fiddly operation.

Though the car in the illustrations is of a remarkably consistent colour, light and objects reflected in the glossy paintwork produce a range of colours and tones.

In the image below, the colour eyedropper has been used to select different parts of the (nominally) yellow paintwork, and to create a small set of swatches – from lemon through primrose yellow and amber to mustard brown.

To replace this range of colours with a single tone would give a very flat, unrealistic effect. You need to alter *all* the tones – an ideal use for the Magic Wand. The amount of colour you select will depend on the Tolerance set. Too low a value will select only a small region of contiguous colour; too large, and you will begin drawing in colour from outside the car.

3 Now, with the car selected you can begin to perform colour changes. Change the hue by using the Hue/Saturation sliders, which can alter the hue through all possible colours. Here are some typical results: the yellow car has become a convincing green and then, by altering the hue slider further, lavender.

Colouring tips

Use this technique to recolour any three-dimensional (or flat, textured) objects. Cars, flowers, even parts of buildings can be modified using this method.

For convincing results, you may need to alter the colour saturation and lightness of the selection when you have chosen your new colour. Be particularly careful when increasing Saturation, as false colour and mottling is easily introduced.

4 Reducing the Saturation (rather than adjusting the hue) produces a silver/grey result.

5 Here's why you shouldn't use a colour fill tool: the same car selection has been filled in using the Paint Bucket tool. Neither convincing nor lifelike.

Using the Clone tool

For many, the Clone tool *is* digital manipulation. This tool – called the Rubber Stamp tool in Adobe applications – can be thought of as a brush that paints with pattern and texture from *another part* of the image.

You can use this technique in two main ways. First, you can copy one part of the image to another to *hide*, or *remove* objects within a scene. Imagine you have a village scene that would, were it not for some satellite dishes and yellow-line road markings, be quintessentially Victorian. You can use the clone tool to remove the lines, dishes and any other contemporary street features. Second, you can *add to* or *enhance* scenes by cloning elements to new positions. You could make a small copse into a forest, for example.

If it is appropriate, you can also clone between images, copying elements from a source or 'donor' image to your current working image.

Setting up and using the clone tool is simple. First, select a brush type and size. You can also adjust the opacity of the clone, normally as a percentage. This will determine how the clone is applied: at low

This sign is easily hidden by cloning nearby areas of grass, bush and wall.

percentages the original image will appear through the cloned overlay. At 100 percent the original pixels are obliterated.

Duplicating important or pronounced elements is another use for the clone tool. In this image, the cross marks the clone-from position, the stamp icon the write-to position.

Clone tool used with 30 percent opacity.

Clone tool used with 100 percent opacity.

Next, you need to set a point, often called the *clone-from* or *source* point, from which you will copy pixels. This is not a fixed point, but rather will move in parallel to your painting movements. It is important, therefore, to ensure that there is sufficient appropriate imagery nearby to effect the clone.

Now, when you use the clone tool, assuming that you have set the tool to Aligned (see right-hand box), you can paint with the texture of your clone-from area to a new area, obscuring the original area under the brush. You can use the opacity (or transparency) control to alter the opacity of the brush (which is sometimes better if a more suble or less obvious effect is sought).

Aligned or non-aligned?

Clone tools often feature the option of setting the tool as Aligned or Non-aligned. To achieve the effect you want, it is important to check that this option is correctly set. In Aligned mode, the sampling point and the writing point maintain their respective positions as you use the tool: the pair move in parallel even if you release the mouse momentarily. In Non-aligned mode, each time the mouse is released and then pressed the sample is taken from the original starting point, irrespective of the current position of the writing point. In the examples below, the same start point was used for both images.

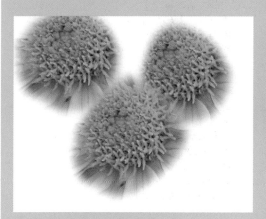

Clone Non-aligned.

Clone Aligned.

Wipeout – using the Clone tool to remove unwanted artefacts

Although some see it as something of a deceit, the Clone tool is ideal for tidying up landscapes that are blotted by less-than-traditional elements. Street signs, telephone and TV cables, power lines and aerials are just some of the features that never seem to be there when you compose shots, but are all too obvious on the print.

the sign. Here, the support poles are vanishing.

A useful way to start is by cleaning up an image, then investigating ways of making further improvement.

The scene above is typical of many: a romantic landscape sweeping down to the sea... only it would look much better without the signs and telegraph poles.

The village sign is easy to deal with. You can use the mixed vegetation hedge that runs behind it to overwrite most of the problems, and the nearby grass for the rest. Select a clone-from point some way from the sign and use it to remove part of

Move the clone-from point (so that the foliage used to overwrite is not an identical copy of the original area) and remove more of the sign.

The sign disappears rapidly. Because the clone-from point has been constantly varied, the new foliage looks entirely convincing.

The process can now be repeated to remove the offending telegraph poles and the car in the distance.

You needn't gloss over details. If there is sufficient material to clone from, you could even go the whole way and remove larger features. In the image above, the road has gone. Removing major areas (particularly when, as here, there is relatively little material to clone from) requires constant relocation of the clone-from point and careful use of clone-from points that are similarly distant to the areas you wish to cover.

Cloning is generally easier when using organic material (as here) to obscure objects. Our eyes tend not to be so sensitive to the slight discrepancies that inevitably occur when foliage is transposed and placed over other foliage. Copying buildings, or parts of buildings, can be more problematic, as slight perspective changes can become apparent.

When removing elements (such as the telegraph poles, wires and TV aerials in this scene) that have sky (or any other continuous colour) for a background, you need to take particular care. It is easy to assume that the sky (particularly when very clear) is a constant colour. It isn't, and cloning can be very obvious (you can see this more easily in the example on the following pages).

Cloning tips

- Watch out for shadows. It is easy to forget that the objects you clone away can cast shadows that also need to be removed.
- If possible, do not clone from an area too close to the one you are writing over. There is a risk of *banding* or *striping* due to the cloned pattern repeating.
- Where the use of the clone tool is obvious, you may be able to blend cloned and original areas by 'adding noise'. The Add Noise filter is a feature of most applications.

Using the Clone tool to rescue a blemished scan

Though scanners (either slide scanners or flatbed, print scanners) represent an excellent way of digitizing images, they can cause problems. Your original images may have defects – dust or scratch marks – that will be all too obviously reproduced. Also, the optical elements of the scanner (for example, the glass plate of a flatbed) could be marked or dusty – no matter how clean your environment, some contamination is inevitable.

Removing such marks is easy once your image is digitized. Take a look at the image above. Bad processing (or possible in-camera damage) has produced tram-line scratch marks. There are also white dust marks (a processing defect), dark dust marks (a scan defect) and even (near the top) a physical scratch. The damage is exacerbated by the clear blue sky.

Tips

If your image is particularly dirty, the Dust and Scratches Filter can be used to remove most blemishes. However, such filters tend to soften the image slightly, so the clone method is to be preferred.

Watch the sky colour carefully in images such as this. Because the variation in tone is very subtle, it is easy to clone an incorrect tone that only becomes obvious when the image is printed. Make sure you clone as closely as possible to the blemish.

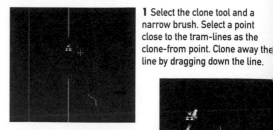
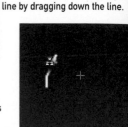

1 Select the clone tool and a narrow brush. Select a point close to the tram-lines as the clone-from point. Clone away the line by dragging down the line.

2 Use the procedure to remove both the black and white dust marks. The blue of the sky varies considerably in tone across the image, so (in this case) ensure that you choose a clone-from point near the defect.

3 To hide marks and the tram-lines where these cross features such as the woodwork, select a clone point that is parallel with the feature. This ensures that both the shape and the texture are preserved.

4 Repeat for all the dust marks and blemishes. The result is a clean image.

Cleaning up a portrait

If cleaning up a clear sky (as in the previous image) is problematic, fixing damage or blemishes in a portrait can be even more so.

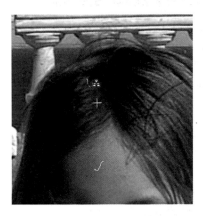

1 Use a fine brush and set the clone tool close to the selection point. To maintain the hair texture, ensure that you clone from hair that runs parallel with that under the mark to be camouflaged.

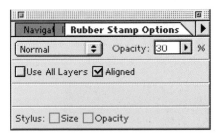

In these cases, you may have to deal with actual skin blemishes. In childrens' portraits, there may be cuts and bruises to smooth over, too.

This image (actually an adjacent frame to the previous one) has already been cleared of scratches and most of the dust marks, but there are still a couple of white marks in the hair and some red spots on the cheeks and chest.

2 Attend to the red spots by cloning the skin colour and texture adjacent to each spot. As the changes in colour across the face are quite marked, set the clone tool's opacity to (say) 30 percent, and clone over the spot repeatedly from different sides of the mark.

Tip

In portraiture, you can sometimes flatter the subject by introducing soft focus. Quite a different effect to blurred focus, soft focus gives a softness to the image without losing the sharpness of details.

This is an excellent dodge for covering minor blemishes without the need to clone each individually. To create a digital soft focus, see page 87.

3 Repeat with all the other marks.

Colour correction and other techniques

Colour correction

It is surprising how often the colour of your images doesn't match that of the original scene. Maybe you used the wrong film type for the lighting conditions; daylight balance film is not suitable for tungsten lighting and vice versa. Some artifical light sources, notably fluorescent tubes, have unusual colour characteristics. Or maybe the vibrant colours you remembered from the original scene have been toned down by the printing process.

Film balanced for tungsten lighting gives daylight shots a cold blue cast.

Tungsten lighting produces a strong amber tint when used with normal daylight film.

a colour between it and its opposite on the colour wheel: red and cyan, magenta and green, blue and yellow.

Begin a correction by selecting the Colour Correction command.

Automated printing processes tend to subdue strong colour casts – assuming that they were unintentional.

Whatever the cause, image editing applications allow subtle – or radical – changes in the colour balance either to correct defects or to introduce dramatic colouring. You'll find the controls under colour balance or colour correction. They work by allowing you to shift the balance of

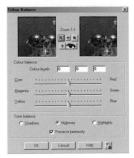

1 Depending on the application, you'll be able to make adjustments either 'live' on the actual image, or using preview boxes in the dialogue box.

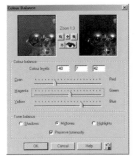

2 When correcting an image with a tungsten orange cast (above right), begin by reducing the red, magenta and yellow components. Move the sliders away from these colours It is hard to be precise about how much to move the sliders. Each case is different, but as a rule of thumb, move the magenta – green slider about half the distance of the other two.

3 Click on the tone balance buttons to perform similar adjustments to the shadows and highlights. Repeat the adjustments.

4 Make a visual assessment of the result. This is easier if there are any areas that are white. If they appear bluish, reduce the blue level slightly, if pink, you may have to reduce the red or magenta components. Check other coloured areas, too, for fidelity. In this example, you could check the wall colour against the original

5 Make any additional corrections.

6 Click OK to apply the corrections to the image. The result (apart from a minor change in the contrast) is very similar to an identical shot taken with film of the correct colour balance (avove right).

Tip

If you use a digital camera, you'll probably have a *white balance* control that automatically corrects for different lighting conditions – even if the lighting comes from mixed sources. Leave this set to *auto* for most applications; you can set it manually if you need to enhance colour casts.

There's no reason why you cannot reverse the colour adjustments described above to *introduce* colour casts into an image. You could, for example, introduce a tungsten-like cast to a fireside scene to impart a feeling of warmth.

Some applications include 'quick fix' features designed to fix colour balance problems instantly. These are useful for correcting colour balance effects caused by incorrect lighting or film type, but will not enhance deliberate colour-cast, such as in a sunset shot. So use quick fix to do the hard work – sorting out the main colour casts – then fine tune the balance as described above.

Adding emphasis to the subject of a portrait

Unless you have the benefit of a large studio, the chances are that most of your portrait work – whether of people or objects – will be made under less than favourable conditions. It is all too easy for distracting backgrounds or competing colours to make their way into your photos and compromise your efforts.

Here are some suggestions for enhancing your subjects:

- Reducing the depth of field.
- Using desaturation for emphasis.
- Creative blurring.

Reducing the depth of field

Photographers have used depth of field to isolate subjects since the earliest days of photography. By focusing on the subject and selecting a wide aperture, those parts of the image in front of and behind the subject become blurred, throwing emphasis on the subject.

Fast films and automatic cameras have put obstacles in the way of this technique. Digital cameras – in general – have made it even more difficult. Most of these cameras have such enormous depth of field that objects from a few inches to infinity are often in reasonable focus.

Here is a simple way to reduce depth of field. It's a useful technique, either for isolating a subject from an otherwise distracting background or simply for increasing the emphasis on the subject.

This portrait (left) was taken with a compact digital camera. The image has impressive, but unwanted, depth of field.

1 Begin with a visual assessment. In this image (as in all portraits of people and animals), the face must be in sharpest focus. If the subject's face were to occupy a larger space in the image, you would need to ensure that at least the eyes were sharp.

2 Select the subject (here 'subject' applies to that part of the image you intend to keep in sharp focus), using an appropriate selection tool. The Lasso (and particularly the Magnetic Lasso) is probably best in this case. Then invert the selection (so that the surroundings are now the selected area).

The sky is the most remote part of this image, and should be that which is most unfocused. The hillside, in depth of field terms, is similarly distant, and will need similar treatment. Intervening objects will need less defocusing, with the bench receiving the least.

3 Choose a Blur filter. Though filters such as Blur and Blur More can be used, if your application has a Gaussian Blur, this gives more control over the degree of blurring. Here, a modest 1-pixel blur has been specified for this first pass.

4 Now select a smaller area, excluding the subject and the bench. This should include the middle distance and sky, as well as any disconnected areas. You can achieve a convincing transition if you select a Feather Radius (in this case around 5), so that there are no discontinuous changes in focus. Use the Gaussian Blur with a radius of around 3 (or use Blur repeatedly) to defocus this area.

5 Finally, select only the sky and the distant hill and apply the Gaussian Blur (set to 6) for a final time. Make the Feather Radius somewhat larger (say 20).

6 The result is an image in which the depth of field is clearly less than in the original, with less background distraction. Careful application of the Blur filters has ensured that the background is not so out of focus that the subject becomes visually detached from it.

Tips

Wherever possible, use natural focal planes when increasing the degree of blurring. By selecting (say) a range of hills beyond the foreground, or even figures at increasing distances, and blurring each group by the same amount, the perspective depth of field effects look much more convincing.

When the subject is in the middle distance, remember to blur foreground objects. For a realistic effect, blurring should be proportionately greater over the smaller distances in the foreground.

Using desaturation for emphasis

There is no doubt that colour is a powerful part of an image. Consider the person with a red hat in a sea of greys and blues. Or the girl with the red coat in the otherwise monochrome *Schindler's List*. Your eye is instantly drawn to the subject, and it attracts an almost unwarranted amount of attention.

You can play the same visual trick with your images, preserving the normal tonality of the subject but decreasing that of the surroundings. Almost any subject is appropriate for this treatment.

Inset below is the portrait from the previous page, this time along with a desaturated version. This is easily achieved by selecting the surroundings (as you did in step 2 on page 61) and choosing Desaturate.

Though the process is otherwise identical, desaturation is less forgiving with regard to selections. Had your original selection been roughly drawn, it would not have been unduly detrimental to the image (except in the eyes of the most pedantic viewer). However, any deviation from the true borders of the subject becomes glaringly obvious when desaturation is applied.

A close look (above) reveals that a small patch of grass (possibly lighter than the rest) was missed in the original selection. As the only remaining patch of green, it is easily seen.

You can use 'local' desaturation tools to fix these. In many applications these take the form of a brush or even a sponge that can be applied to the offending area. Only the colour is removed; the image remains otherwise unaffected (below).

Once you have selected – and desaturated – your background, you needn't stop there. You could apply any other effect you like to add emphasis to your subject. In the image above, a Line Art filter has been used to make the surroundings look as if they were drawn with a technical pen. As ever, when using such effects, be mindful of your subject; the aim of this process is to add emphasis, not to distract attention.

Creative blurring

Hidden amongst the sober and workmanlike tools in the Blur toolset, you may find an unusual offering. With names such as Zoom blur and Motion blur, this is not a Blur tool in the accepted photographic sense, but it's very useful for providing emphasis. In Photoshop or Photoshop Elements, the Zoom blur is an option in the Radial blur filter.

Zoom blur first. Its effect is rather like that achieved when a camera is set to a moderately long exposure and the lens zoomed during the exposure. The image appears to *explode* from the page. It can be difficult to view – the movement of the subject and surroundings is not easy on the eye, but with the right subjects it can work well. Moving subjects are ideal, especially if coming towards the camera. Action shots also work well. Here's how to get the best from it:

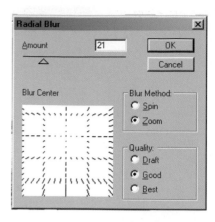

2 Open the Zoom blur dialogue box. Move the Zoom centre position to the chosen point. Set the Blur amount. You'll probably have to try a few different settings until you get the best for your subject. Set it too high, and it will be hard to make out anything in your image; too low, and the effect may just look like camera shake.

3 Apply the effect. If the subject is quite small as a proportion of the total image area, there's no need to make a selection before applying.

1 Open your image and perform any other manipulations (e.g. cropping or colour correction) first. Decide where you want your Zoom to begin. Normally, if your subject is a person, the centre should be that subject's face.

4 If the subject is larger, or there is too much blurring on, say, the subject's face, select this first and then invert the selection before applying the Zoom.

Zoom filters are excellent for creating dramatic motion effects, especially when used, as here, head on to a subject. They also provide a useful technique for drawing attention to a subject within a scene.

5 Here's the final image. Subtle use of the Zoom has given it a strong feeling of motion.

The Radial Blur filter can create a variety of effects, depending on the degree to which it is used. At a very low setting, the impression can just be blurred – rather like the effect of a cheap camera lens, where the centre of the image is sharp but the surroundings increasingly less so). Too high a setting will blur the surroundings to such a degree that the context of the image – the subject in its environment – is lost.

Combining effects

You can combine effects to produce added emphasis. Here, selective blurring is introduced, followed by a vignette, both as add-ons to the technique discussed earlier. Such effects are ideal for portraits of animals, and can even be used to give unimaginative childrens' portraits extra appeal.

Freehand vignettes are an ideal way of cutting out distractions. By fading the surroundings, you can ease away any superfluous elements which you might not be able to remove by other methods, such as cloning.

This technique is also useful for creating image collages. The softened edges help to blend adjacent images.

1 Draw a rough, feathered selection loosely around your subject using the lasso tool. Leave a gap between the selection and the subject slightly larger than the feather distance.

2 Invert the selection and apply a Gaussian Blur. Set the blur level quite high (40 – 50).

3 Draw an oval vignette around the subject, including some of the blurred surroundings. Invert the selection and press delete (here a background colour has been selected sampled from the image's surroundings).

4 The result. Blurring and vignette have reduced the prominence of the surroundings, concentrating the emphasis on the subject.

Above, the Lasso tool has been used to follow the broad outline of the subject.

Creating a loose vignette around the subject (right) is a way of removing distractions without totally removing the subject from the surroundings.

Tip

Using a background colour sampled from the scene's surroundings (as here, with the vignette) helps to add emphasis to the subject. A complementary colour can be distracting.

There is no rule that a vignette has to be oval, circular or even rectangular. If a subject suggests an alternate shape, even if freehand, use it.

Sharpening images

There is a widely-held misconception that image manipulation is good for sharpening blurred photographs. The truth is that while a computer can do most things to an image, rescuing a blurred shot remains impossible. When an image is out of focus, little of the detail – and none of the fine detail – is recorded. No amount of manipulation can bring this back. However, image manipulation applications do feature Sharpen tools that can be used to add sharpness to an image that was not critically sharp in the first place.

Remember that while these tools can improve an already good shot, used without care, they can compromise overall quality. Often, you do not enhance an image by digital sharpening, but rather make its digital origins all too obvious.

Sharpening tools work by identifying edges in your image. In an unsharp image, such boundaries tend to be comparatively wide and soft. These transitions are then narrowed, to give the perception of sharpness.

Sharpen filters

You may find many Sharpen filters in your application. A typical set might include Sharpen, Sharpen More, Sharpen Edges and Unsharp mask. Sharpen More applies a sharpening effect about four times as great as Sharpen. Both are somewhat crude in their effects, as is Sharpen Edges. In each case, there is a tendency to introduce artefacts that, at best, reduce contrast and give a flat image. Worse still, they can introduce very obvious artefacts (for a definition, see the Glossary).

This image is sharp, but not critically so.

Applying Sharpen More twice produces an image that lacks both the tonality and contrast of the original.

Closer inspection of the image shows more serious damage. Image artefacts have caused serious degradation – both those which were present originally, but suppressed, and those due to the sharpening procedure itself.

Unsharp mask

Despite the name (which originated from a traditional photographic darkroom technique) the Unsharp mask provides a controllable way of image sharpening. See the next two pages.

The Unsharp mask dialogue box features three controls: Amount (for the amount of sharpening applied), Radius (the pixel distance over which sharpening is performed) and Threshold (the brightness level over which pixels need to be to be sharpened). Accurate sharpening requires a subtle adjustment of all three.

In some applications (such as Paintshop Pro, shown right), the controls governing sharpening are named Radius, Strength and Clipping respectively

1 (top) This image is reasonably sharp, but could benefit from a little further work.

2 (middle) Open the Unsharp Mask dialogue box and set some nominal parameters. A useful starting point is: Amount, 200 percent, Radius, 2, Threshold, 1. The results are good, but almost too good. You've sharpened the eyes and lips, but also sharpened the skin texture, which for a woman's face is generally regarded as unflattering.

3 (bottom) Reduce the Amount to 100 percent and increase the Threshold to 5. Not only are you reducing the effect, but also limiting where it will act. Now the skin is much softer – a far more flattering effect.

Using the Unsharp Mask is an inexact science. Though there can be guide figures for the parameters, a degree of trial and error is required to find the optimum values. (*See* facing page for a range of Unsharp Mask adjustments and their effects).

Because sharpening tends to exaggerate artefacts (or introduce new ones), subsequent image manipulations such as tonal changes, saturation increases or adjustments can make these more prominent. It's a good idea, then, to make sharpening your final adjustment prior to printing or saving your image. Mode changes (say from RGB to CMYK) can make sharpening more obvious, so again, sharpen *after* any such changes.

Examine your image once sharpened, both overall and in detail, to assess the effect. A sensible precaution (as with any major image manipulations) is to work on a copy of your image so that you can revert to the original should you later discover a problem.

Tips

In portraits, you aim to limit the amount of fine detail (such as skin texture) but sharpen the larger and more pronounced elements (such as eyes and lips). If you were trying to sharpen a landscape (or, more particularly, a cityscape), you might want to retain as much fine detail as possible. In these cases you would set (as a starting point) your parameters as: Threshold, 0 (to sharpen everything); Radius, 2; Amount, 150 percent.

Unsharp Mask settings   Unsharp Mask used with the following Amount,
Radius and Threshold parameters.

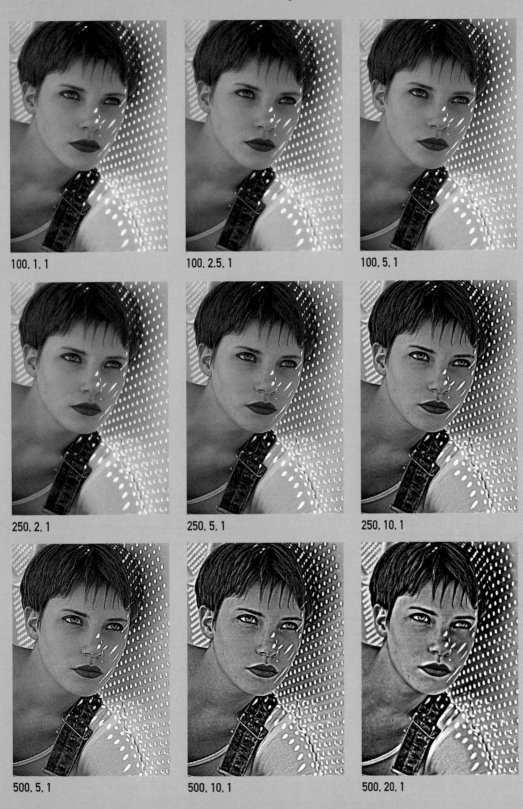

100, 1, 1

100, 2.5, 1

100, 5, 1

250, 2, 1

250, 5, 1

250, 10, 1

500, 5, 1

500, 10, 1

500, 20, 1

Hand colouring a black and white print

Before colour photography existed and, for a time, when it was not a credible medium for the general marketplace, hand colouring of images was commonplace. The process had its origins far earlier, when printing methods permitted only a single ink colour: laborious hand colouring was the only way to reproduce colour.

A hand-coloured image has a distinctive look and is easily recreated digitally.

1 Select a black and white image. Don't choose anything too complex for a first attempt. The process is like painting by numbers, so it makes sense to have a limited number of colours and a small range of areas. An image like this is ideal. If your image is in greyscale mode, convert it to RGB (colour).

3 Select a soft-edged brush type, a colour, and begin colouring your image. With these mode settings, do not worry about colour build-up if you repeatedly colour across the same area.

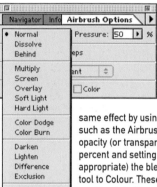

2 Hand colouring uses translucent water colour inks – rather than opaque paints. We can achieve the same effect by using a painting tool such as the Airbrush, setting the opacity (or transparency) to 50 percent and setting (where appropriate) the blend mode of the tool to Colour. These settings allow you to paint with a chosen colour, but not to obliterate any of the original image.

4 When the first colour area is complete, move on to the next. image contains a range of grey need not worry about altering t tone. For example, one tone of was used for each plant here, full range of shades results fro colouring.

5 Don't feel you have to colour everything: the best results oft come from a limited palette.

Tips

If you don't have any black and white images, you can create your own from any colour image by desaturating a colour print. Depending on the image, you may need to alter the contrast to get an acceptable base.

Surprisingly, you still get a worthwhile result if you are slightly inaccurate with your painting. It is a peculiarity of human vision that we 'see' a properly coloured and filled object even when there are uncoloured or miscoloured elements. But don't use this physiological effect as an excuse for poor workmanship!

Creating a duotone

A duotone is an alternative way of toning a black and white image. Unlike conventional tinting techniques (where the toning colour replaces the blacks and greys), a duotone adds a single additional colour.

To create a duotone you'll need to begin with a greyscale image. If your image is colour, change the mode to greyscale. As this mode change permanently removes the colour information from the image, it makes sense to work on a copy of the image.

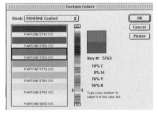

1 Select Duotone from the mode options. The duotone dialogue box will open.

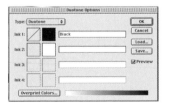

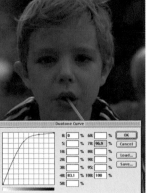

2 By default, the base ink colour shown will be black. Click on the ink 2 window to add a second colour. As duotones are used extensively in the printing world, the colour choices often include the precisely-defined Pantone ® colours. Choose one of these, or select the colour picker to mix your own.

3 Next, click on the curve box (to the left of the ink swatch box) to open the duotone curves dialogue box. By default, the graph will be a simple diagonal.

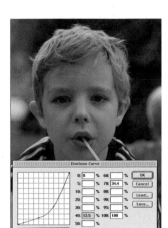

4 These graphs represent the tones in the image with the normal 255 tones converted to a simple percentage. Dragging parts of the curve above the diagonal will darken the colour relative to the original; dropping it below will lighten it. Subtle duotones will result from lowering the line.

5 When you have a curve that gives colours you are happy with, apply the levels and save.

A warm landscape

Duotones can be used to give warm and cool effects. You can use them to warm up a landscape, say, more subtly and effectively than conventional toning permits. For this example, a warm brown has been selected for the second colour and applied with a slightly negative (that is, lighter colour) duotone curve.

Tritones and quadtones

Adding a third or even a fourth colour to an original greyscale image produces a tritone or quadtone respectively. The additional colours could contrast with the original (for strong colour effects) or be subtly different. If the latter, very soft and gentle colour gradations are possible.

The result – warmed up, but still essentially a monochrome image.

1 The original monochrome (greyscale) image.

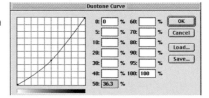

2 A second, warm colour is selected.

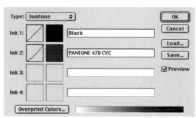

3 To lighten the application of the new colour, the curve is adjusted

Complementary colours have been used in this tritone.

Why duotones?

Duotones create interesting graphic effects, but do they have a serious purpose? Yes. Photographers produce images that, converted to a digital file, have 255 levels of grey. But the printing process used for books and magazines rarely offers many more than 50. To extend the tonal range, a supplementary technique is required – and this is duotone. Adding a second colour requires a further printing plate, but also adds another 50 levels, making the tonal changes more subtle. For even better results, *tritones* (three colours) and even *quadtones* (four colours) can be used.

Setting the blend to grey gives this quadtone a range of very subtle tones.

Extreme duotones

Though duotones are designed for adding subtle gradations, adjusting the curves graph in extreme ways can produce wacky effects. With negative curves, results such as this are possible.

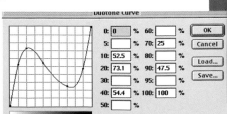

Removing red-eye

Red-eye is a common problem with flash exposures, particularly if the flashgun is mounted on the camera or flash is used in dark conditions. The effect is

Red-eye removal tool

Found in some, but not all, applications, this is nothing more than a specialized desaturation brush that you drag across the affected eyes. Unlike conventional desaturation tools (which desaturate all colours in the image), the Redeye tool desaturates only red.

You need to use the tool precisely. Make sure that the brush covers only the red pupil; as the iris and skin already have red components, overzealous use can produce localized monochrome results. This is clearly shown in the illustration above.

Dedicated redeye tools are usually best for shots that contain many red eyes, such as a party group, rather than individual shots where you need to work more precisely.

caused by flash light reflecting off the subject's retina at the back of the eye (this is reddish in colour). You can avoid or reduce the problem by using bounce flash or by moving the flashgun some way from the lens axis, but often enough, the damage is already done, and chances are the occasion – typically a childrens' party – can't be repeated. However, help is at hand in your digital toolbox, which offers several easy ways to restore normal colour to the eyes.

Selection tools

Greater accuracy and, ultimately, greater authenticity, can be achieved by a manual correction.

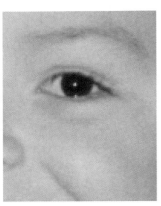

1 Begin by zooming in on an eye.

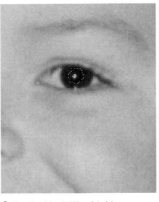

2 Use the Magic Wand (with a tolerance of around 20) to select the red parts of the eye). Don't worry if the white highlight is also included.

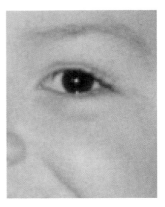

3 Use the Desaturate tool to remove the red.

Tips

Sometimes the redeye is so bright that, when desaturated, the pupil is a light grey colour.

Depending on how light the grey, increasing the contrast of the selected area may make the pupil colour more authentic. In extreme cases it might be necessary to use a dark grey paint colour to fill the selection. In this case, ensure that any white highlight in the eye is *not* part of the selection.

Watch out for similar effects if you use flash to take pictures of animals and pets. Dogs are prone to exhibit greeneye, and cats whiteeye or yelloweye.

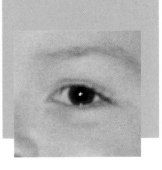

4 Repeat for the second eye (and any others).

Adding impact using grain and noise

I f you've worked with traditional photographic film – rather than digital media – you'll know how much effort film companies put into making the grain almost invisible. Even fast emulsions now boast fine grain characteristics.

It might seem odd, then, to introduce grain deliberately in order to add impact. But grain – or rather, the grittiness it imparts – is useful for adding character and mood. Grain works well on *hard* subjects: cityscapes, industrial scenes, rugged landscapes and portraits of men. It can – conversely – even be used with care to give certain shots a romantic feel.

Grain works best when it does not have to compete with vibrant colours; images with subdued colour – even monchrome – are best. The Victorian harbour scene pictured here is suitable.

2 Select Add Grain. On some applications, the Add Noise feature or Noise filter give a similar effect. They just add grain to the image, allowing you to monitor the amount using the preview window. Selecting Monochromatic produces grain without the random colour that is otherwise generated. Make sure that this is selected if your images are monochrome.

3 Apply the grain.

1 Start by desaturating the colours. Here, total desaturation has been avoided, leaving a hint of the orignal colours.

4 As grain tends to flatten the contrast in an image, you may find it appropriate to increase the image contrast at the start if your original image is flat. Here, the image is fully desaturated.

Your application may have alternative grain options that give effects quite different from the standard film grain effect. This option (in Photoshop) is called Vertical Grain. It creates a distressed, worn look to this sepia-toned version of the image.

Adding grain can sometimes add anomalous colours. Sometimes this can add to the pictorial value of the image, but at other times you may wish to suppress it. Use the Monochromatic button in the appropriate dialogue box (if available) to add monochromatic noise to a colour image.

For the image below the original colours, already somewhat muted, have been retained, and a conventional grain pattern applied. The result is particularly successful, largely because it recreates the effect of early colour photographs

Adding noise to this image and then tinting it blue turns it into a powerful graphic image.

Tip

Don't overdo grain. Too much, and the image will simply be too flat.

Jpeg tip

The JPEG compression technique introduces unsightly rectangular artefacts that become pronounced when the image is enlarged. Adding a little grain – if the subject permits – is a way of camouflaging this.

A gentle touch

Because grain has a softening, flattening effect, you can use it to give an ethereal, romantic atmosphere to informal portraits and landscapes.

On the wedding photograph above, for instance, you might use the Add Grain feature to give a romantic quality and,

conveniently, to soften the somewhat distracting jumble of plants near the camera.

By softening the image (using a Blur filter) before applying the grain, you can get a halo effect around the highlights – particularly effective on the bride's dress (see below).

Painting with light – and dark

Of all conventional darkroom techniques, dodge and burn are possibly the most well known. Dodging (reducing the exposure in selected areas to lighten them) and burning (increasing the exposure to give a darker, more intense result) can give dramatic interest to an otherwise lacklustre image.

Digital burns and dodges are, of course, integral to most applications. You can take a brush (any one from your palette) and use it to lighten or darken the image. As with other brush-based tools, you can alter the intensity of the application (normally called exposure) between 0 and 100 percent. You can also choose which range of tones you work in, selecting from shadows, midtones and highlights. Choosing shadows will only affect the dark tones in the image, highlights the lighter tones, and midtones the midtones, so you have an almost limitless range of control.

This sunset shown to the left is typical of shots that, because they are shot into the light and contain large areas of shadow, have too much contrast. The photographer saw a much more interesting scene when he took this shot.

1 Try to view the shot in the way your eyes would have perceived it. For example, you would have seen the detail in the sky and the rocks around the foreshore. Take some time working out which areas need burning and which need dodging. Here, those to be dodged are shown with a blue overlay, those to be burned, red.

2 Select the Dodge tool and set an exposure of 50 percent. Use a soft-edged brush to apply the effect. This will prevent any hard boundaries. Begin sweeping across the areas to be dodged. The action of the Dodge tool tends to be cumulative, so do not pause during your strokes.

3 Continue dodging until you've achieved the desired lightness. Notice how colour, lost in the original image, becomes visible again.

4 Dramatic sunset restored.

Tips

It is advisable to work with low exposure settings first. High exposure settings (with Burn, particularly) can emphasise and exaggerate the colour in an image.

Though it sounds contradictory, dodge shadows (like those above) by selecting the highlights option. You'll achieve more subtle effects because the real highlights treated. These cloudscapes illustrate the action of the tools more clearly.

The original image.

Burn tool, shadows selected.

Dodge tool, highlights selected.

Both tools used.

The hand and the lolly

If you've wondered about the curious icons sometimes used to denote Burn and Dodge, they too hail from the days of the traditional darkroom. The lolly on a stick – the Dodge tool – represents the small cardboard mask used to shield parts of the image. It would be attached to a piece of wire.

The hand – for the Burn tool – relates to the use of hands (and arms in some cases) that are used to cover most of the image to allow the unprotected areas to burn through.

The high-key portrait

3 Isolate the subject by dodging away the surroundings. Depending on the setting, you may consider it appropriate to remove all the background, or simply to make it lighter than the subject. Here, the background has been faded, in much the same way as in a feathered vignette. To finish, adjust Levels to further shift the tonal range towards light rather than dark. A couple of catchlights (highlights on the eyes) have been painted on here in order to add sparkle.

High-key is the term used to describe the effect of shifting the tonal balance of a photograph from what might be described as normal towards lighter tones. The result is a delicate, airy effect, ideal for feminine portraiture.

Ideally, the effect is created both by careful lighting and subsequent darkroom work. Here, a high-key portrait is created using just dodge and burn skills.

Take away the colour

Burning has an unfortunate tendency to exaggerate and even distort colour, so don't forget that high-key works equally well in monochrome. Desaturate your image before editing, or change the image mode to greyscale (below).

1 Use the Dodge tool (with a low exposure, around 20 percent) to lighten the eyes. Pay particular attention to the whites and the irises. If there are teeth in the image, use the same tool to whiten these too. If the lips are a little lost, use the Burn tool to darken them slightly.

2 Using the Dodge tool again (and this time choosing a relatively large brush), lighten the face. Pay attention to the direction of the light, so that natural shading is not smoothed away, merely lightened.

Tips

Don't blur the layer image too much. The aim is to soften the highlights rather then distend them.

A soft focus portrait

Soft focus effects are ideal for exploring layers. (Soft focus, by the way, does not mean blurred. The point of soft focus is to retain the image's sharpness while softening it so that a halo surrounds all the highlights.)

1 Choose the image you want to soften. Crop the image and, if appropriate, emphasise the subject by blurring the surroundings. You can do this digitally (*see* pages 60-61).

In a camera, soft focus is often achieved by using specialized filters such as the renowned Hasselblad Softar® range. On the face of it, these are clear filters with plane glass that record a sharp image. However, small blisters on the filter's surface also soften the image. The size and number of these blisters (which vary from filter to filter) determine the degree of softening.

The good news (if you have ever had to enquire about the price of a Softar filter) is that you can achieve an infinitely variable amount of softening digitally.

2 Make a *duplicate layer* of this image. An exact copy of the image will be created. Select the duplicate layer and apply the Gaussian Blur filter to blur the whole layer. A modest setting (say 20 per cent) is usually enough.

3 Now vary the Opacity (or Transparency) of the layer. This allows the original (sharp) image to show through your blurred layer. At zero opacity, the image is completely sharp; at 100 percent, it is blurred. Make a nominal setting of 50 percent and consider the result.

Looking at the image in close-up shows the difference between a blurred and a softened image. In the blurred image, there is softness but no detail. The softened image preserves all but the finest detail, and combines it with a soft glow. The finest detail that is lost tends to be that which is least flattering – skin texture and skin blemishes, for example.

'Soft' is not blurred

Blurred image.

Softened image.

Pasting into selections

The Paste Into command lets you paste new images *into* selections made on a main image. You can use this to create novel frame effects using photos of conventional picture frames, or other, less obvious sources.

1 Begin by selecting – or taking – an image that will provide a frame. This is a picture frame photographed against a fabric background.

2 Select the picture area (the Polygonal Lasso is ideal), then press delete to check the shape of the area selected.

3 Open the image you want to paste into the frame. Select the entire image (or an appropriate crop). Here's the image created in the vignette example (*see* page 66).

4 Check that the pixel dimensions of this image match that of the space it will be pasted into. If not, adjust the size appropriately (see page 46 for details of altering size and resolution).

5 With the image selected, choose Copy from the edit menu to copy the image to the clipboard.

6 Make the frame image the active image and select Paste Into from the edit menu. Paste Into will paste your clipboard selection into the frame selected on this image.

When you use Paste Into, the image you paste into the selection is held in a separate layer. So, if you need to, you can move this image around relative to the frame to get the best position.

The secret garden

Here's another way of using Paste Into. You'll take this *trompe l'oeil* doorway and add a 'real' scene beyond.

1 As before, select the doorway. The rectangular shape calls for the Polygonal Lasso.

2 Check the image for any intrusions such as – here – the ivy growing around the doorframe, and ensure that they are added to the selection. The Magic Wand (in the 'Add-to Selection' mode) was helpful here.

4 Select the image and use Paste Into.

3 Choose the image to paste into the scene and adjust its size. If you are unsure about adjusting image sizes, select this image and paste on to the frame image to get an approximate idea of the relative sizes.

5 Here, an alternate image has been pasted into the doorway to create the illusion of a garden beyond.

Stamp

With this technique, even the most unlikely of images can be used. Below, a stamp was photographed using the macro setting on a digital camera.

1 The stamp window was selected and the queen's head and '31' removed from the selection so that only the picture made the final selection.

2 This photo of a dog was selected for pasting into the selection.

3 The dog is pasted into position. The resulting image is quite convincing.

4 Alternatively you could select the queen's head and the '31' and alter their colour to make them stand out more against the background. Changing the colour to grey, for example, makes them more prominent.

Perspective control

Perspective effects – where parallel vertical or horizontal lines appear to converge as they get more distant from the viewpoint – are often used for dramatic effect, as here, to emphasise scale and height.

To a greater or lesser degree, similar distortion is present in all images where the camera and object are not precisely parallel: just a modest tilt can produce visible distortion that only becomes marked when a vertical straight-edge is placed against the scene.

The traditional method of correcting perspective distortion is to use an expensive (and fiddly) perspective control lens, or, even more complex, an adjustable large-format camera.

1 Assess the perspective defects in your image. Work out how the true vertical relates to the image vertical. Here, the difference is indicated in red.

2 Select the Distort tool. This provides a selection around your object whose corners and sides can be moved to counter the perspective. If you are correcting converging verticals, consider lowering the height of the image slightly, to prevent it becoming unduly tall. (*contd over*)

3 Apply the distortion. Here's the corrected image, with plumb-straight verticals.

Digital image editing provides a more elegant and (because it can be applied retrospectively) timely solution. You can use dedicated perspective tools (such as Crop In Perspective in Photoshop, or Perspective Distort in Photo-Paint), or simply use Distortion tools. Whatever method you choose (or whatever your application will permit), the process is essentially the same.

Tip

Perspective control invariably leads to an image that is more tightly cropped to the main subject; so if you plan to correct perspective, make sure that you add a wider border around the subject when taking the shot than you might otherwise.

Getting creative

Perspective correction is generally regarded as a *fixing* tool – that is, it is, one used to correct deficiencies within an original image. But it also offers creative opportunities. Because such tools enable distorted elements to be converted to rectilinear form, you can, for example, use them to extract imagery from within an existing image.

1 Look through your images and seek, for example, a painting on a wall or a building façade. The painting in the image above is an ideal subject – and might make a great image in its own right.

2 Use the Perspective or Distort tools, as before, but this time carefully drag the corner points to the corners of your subject.

3 Complete the command. Because the software doesn't know the original proportions of the image, you may need to correct the length-to-height ratio. (This often requires a 'best guess'.)

4 Make any further adjustments that may be necessary to render the new image convincing. The contrast and brightness will probably need adjusting from the values that were appropriate in the original image.

Tips

When extracting an image, as here, the new image will be – in definition terms – smaller than the original and unsuitable for the same degree of enlargement.

The process of straightening out the original selection tends to involve adding, removing and redefining pixels. So there is a risk of the image becoming soft. Further manipulation (such as using an Unsharp Mask) may be necessary to bring out the best in the image.

Where you are cropping the image to an area significantly smaller than the original, the resulting crop may be of poor resolution unless you start with an image of very high resolution.

If you are correcting vertical or horizontal lines you can use grid or guide overlays to ensure that your results are spot-on. These are offered in most applications and enable a graph-like grid or individual line to be placed over the image. The guides are often the more useful option, as they can be placed precisely over those parts of the image that you are attempting to align.

Layers and filters

Levels, curves and histograms

L evels, curves and histograms represent an area of digital imaging that many shy away from in the mistaken belief that they are complex or esoteric. But give them a chance and you'll find them your best friends.

When you acquire a digital image, whether from a scanner, Picture CD or digital camera, the results can be less than ideal. Though the image may look OK on screen, it might just be lacking that punch that transforms a good picture into a great one.

Image editors offer a range of tools for improving such raw material. Some are basic and involve no more than a button push or menu selection. These include Auto Enhance, Fix Photo and Auto Levels – 'magic cure-alls' which in many cases are pretty successful. They change the colour, tonal distribution and contrast range towards those of an idealized print – one with average tones, average contrast and a mix of colours. So long as your image 'works' under these conditions, the fix will work.

But what of those images that don't conform? For these, a second range of corrective tools comes into play. In particular, the Histogram and

Levels commands tell you much about the nature of an image and allow you to make effective corrections.

When you first see a Histogram, you may well ask how an image with millions of colours can be represented by so trivial a graph? In fact, the Histogram is simply a representation of how the tones correspond to the 256 tones that *should* comprise the image. The shape and population of the curve (i.e. the way it is filled) tell much about the image, as seen in the following examples.

Histograms explained
Three images, three histograms.

In this night scene, dark tones dominate. There are very few areas of light and intermediate tone. The Histogram shows this: the curve is skewed towards the left, with the majority of the tones in the black and dark grey region.

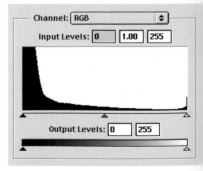

Where the tones are more broadly distributed, the Histogram curve has no obvious shape. However, a practised eye can attribute minor peaks in the curve to characteristics of the scene.

Exploring levels

So, a histogram gives an overview of the tonal make-up of the image. How does this information help us create a *better* image? Now the Levels menu comes into its own. In many applications (and many descriptive manuals), Levels and Histogram are almost synonymous. In fact, the term Levels is used to denote tonal levels in the Histogram, but is usually applied to a Histogram command that permits modification of the Histogram. Here is a typical Levels dialogue box:

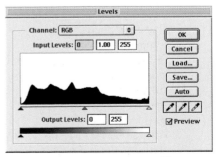

A high-key image in which there are virtually no blacks or dark tones gives a curve closely drawn to the lighter (i.e. the right-hand) part of the Histogram.

Note the sliders beneath the Histogram. The one on the left represents the black point in the image; normally, this position would define the black tones. The white point, to the far right, corresponds to the position of white.

95

Images often don't have a full tonal range, particularly if they were scanned from a print, or perhaps sourced from a Photo CD. Histograms of such images will not extend from black point to white.

The Photo CD image shown here is typical. Though there is a *fair* range of tonal values, they stop abruptly at around 220, rather than 256. This is despite the fact there are obvious areas of white and nearly-white tones in the image.

By moving the right slider to the end of the Histogram curve, the image (viewed live) develops a more extensive tonal range. The whites become brighter.

If you apply the new Levels setting and then look at the Histogram again, you will find that the tonal values have been stretched to fill the 256 levels available.

Don't be too concerned if, as here, the Histogram looks a little disjointed, with clear lines appearing periodically across the distribution. This is an artefact of the 'stretching', wherein certain intermediate

levels are left empty. As only discrete values are so affected, there is no undue cause for concern.

Note that is is quite acceptable to remove one or two levels of data at either end of the Histogram when adjusting the spectrum. Losing around (say) 0.5 percent will remove extraneous (and sometimes erroneous) levels that sometimes populate these parts of the Histogram.

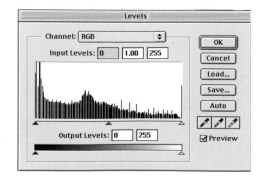

Conversely, this old scanned print has no true dark tones, and to a lesser extent, no true whites.

Moving both sliders to the respective start/end of the histogram curve delivers a much better image.

Histogram tips

Use the middle slider – the grey Input Levels slider – to alter the midtones in an image. Use it if your image has an otherwise perfect distribution, or if alterations to the black or white points have affected the image. Drag the slider to the right to darken, to the left to lighten.

As a rule of thumb, the middle slider can be placed so that the black area of the histogram to the left of it is roughly similar to the right's. Then make fine adjustments based on this rough placement.

Automatic level-adjusting commands (such as Auto Levels) tend to make changes based only on white and black points. After using such commands, check for midtone balance, and adjust as required.

Curves

In photography, an input-output curve maps the sensitivity/response of a film against image density. This is notionally a straight, 45-degree line graph with one-to-one correspondence, though in practice, the inconsistencies of film emulsion cause slight curves and bows.

In digital editing software, the Curves command and the Curves dialogue boxes do the same thing. But while film has a fixed response, you can change the curve of your digital image, thereby altering its characteristics. Manipulations of the Curves graph can create other interesting effects as will be seen later (page 158, Sabattier Effect).

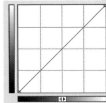

When first opened. the Curves dialogue box features a 45-degree line graph.

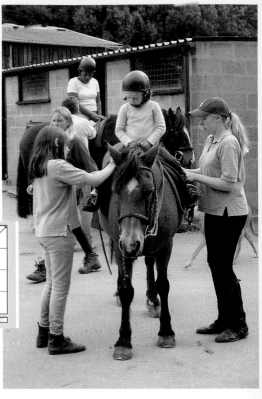

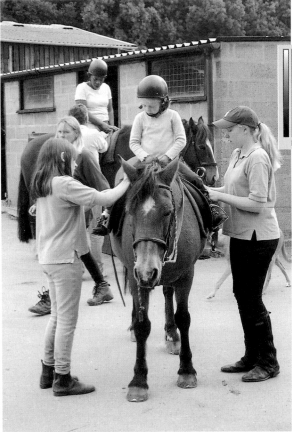

Lifting the curve (by clicking on and dragging the line) above the 45-degree position will give a brighter image.

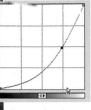

Depressing the curve below the 45-degree position results in a darker image.

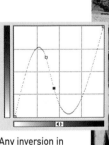

Any inversion in the curve (any segment of the line given a negative, downhill slope) produces wacky, psychedelic colours.

Working with Layers

L ayers are so important that it is hard to imagine working without them. They are an easy means of stacking image elements and even digitally created effects. They allow you to 'pull your images apart' and alter the content of any Layer without affecting other parts of the image.

Different applications have somewhat different names – and rules – for Layers, typically in terms of how many you can have and how they interact. In Corel's CorelDRAW and Photo-Paint the equivalent of Layers is Floating Objects.

Adjustment Layers and image protection

A specialized Layer, often called an Adjustment Layer, lets you float image adjustments within a scene.

This Layer contains only instructions – such as alterations to levels, contrast or colour balance – to be applied to Layers below, rather than to pixels comprising part of the image. Those Layers affected by the Adjustment Layer are not physically changed; turning the Adjustment Layer off or removing it entirely will return those Layers to their normal state. So Adjustment Layers are a useful way of applying changes without making them permanent. Your original image remains safe. Photo-Paint's Lenses are equivalent to Adjustment Layers.

Saving Layers

If you want to save a multi-layer image, you will probably have to use your image editing application's native file format (such as PSD for Photoshop).

Using one of the more portable formats (JPEG, for example) will flatten the image and prevent any subsequent layer-based adjustments.

The layered image

Shown on the page opposite is the type of layering that you might see when creating an image.

ANTIQUES FAIR

Read from the bottom up:

The text was added next, and appears as the top Layer in the stack. After creating this, Drop Shadow and Inner Shadow effects were added to make the text more clearly visible.

Next, a Pattern Fill Adjustment Layer was created. This is not currently seen as part of the image: note that the 'eye' icon to the left of this Layer is not visible.

The large brooch has been selected and a Colour Balance Adjustment Layer created. This is shown by the Mask icon and the Colour Balance icon.

An identical copy, made so that any changes can be mixed with the original later.

The original background image.

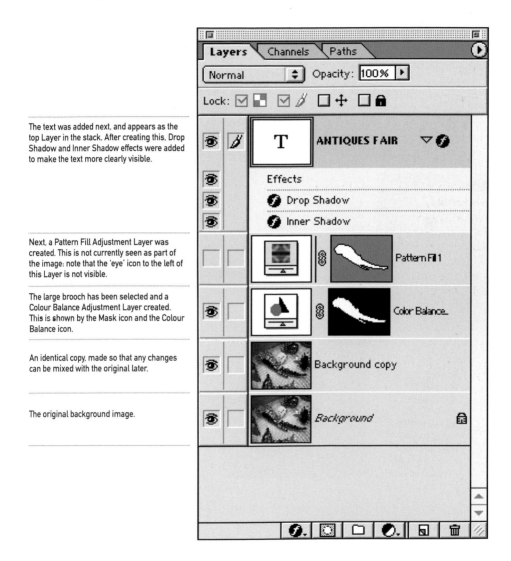

Creating temporary Masks

Temporary masks – those not designed to be stored as part of the image structure – are useful tools for creating, altering and refining selections. Sometimes called Quick Masks, they allow almost any tool (even filter effects) to modify the mask. Here's how you can use a Quick Mask to modify a selection:

This turtle is potentially a problematic subject: too many tones make the Magic Wand unsuitable; low-contrast edges mean the Magnetic Lasso will have an uphill task.

1 Even so, use the Magnetic Lasso to describe the edge. Some errors are inevitable: here, the feet have been incorrectly selected, and in a few places, parts of the background grass have been included in the selection.

2 Switch to Quick Mask mode. A red overlay appears across the masked areas (i.e. those included in the selection). The errors are more obvious in this view.

3 Zoom in on one of the problem areas. Here, you need to add the remainder of the turtle's foot to the selection by removing that part of the mask that covers it.

Quickmask tips

When removing a mask, it is often difficult to remove it just to the image boundary: you can often get faster and more accurate results by removing it beyond the boundary and then painting it back to the edge.

You can also use the mask technique to tidy selection edges. The edges created by selection tools such as the Magnetic Lasso are often jagged. Using a fine brush in Quick Mask mode, can smooth these to follow the true boundary.

Switching to Quick Mask mode is useful when using the Magic Wand on mottled surfaces. In such cases, the wand may fail to select some pixels and this only becomes obvious after a change has been applied. Scrubbing the area with a brush in Quick Mask mode will ensure that any such points are absorbed into the selection.

4 To edit the mask you now need to select a tool. A Paintbrush, with a hard edge, would be ideal. Painting with black adds to the masked area. Painting with white removes masking. Here, white paint has been used to remove the mask (note that painting with shades of grey produces a semi-transparent mask, ideal for feathering or applying gentle effects).

5 The mask has been both added to and subtracted from here to define the outline better. (If you make any mistakes, or remove too much mask, simply reverse the colour.)

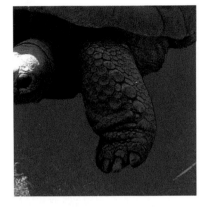

6 Work your way around the selection until you are happy that the boundaries of the mask correspond with those of the intended selection. Switch back to normal mode in order to review your selection.

Origins of the Mask?

The origins of the mask are found in the printing industry, where a rubberized compound was physically painted on to film in order to block further exposure of the selected elements. This compound was known as *Rubylith*, and its red colour prevented the transmission of the ultra-violet light used to develop plates. In digital imaging, red is therefore a traditional choice for the mask, but it is also the most visible on the majority of images. You can, however, change it should you (say) be working on an image that contains an high percentage of red.

7 Here, for clarity, the selection has been copied to a new layer to show how well the mask has worked.

Creating photographic edges using the Quick Mask

Photographic edges add a useful finishing touch, especially effective on pictures for display in clip frames and on those to be pasted into documents and brochures.

1 Open the edited and cropped image. Adding the edge should be the final stage.

2 Use the Rectangular Marquee to select the image, leaving a 5 to 10 percent border around all sides. Switch to Quick Mask. You'll see the border turn red as the mask is applied.

3 Now apply a filter. It will work only on the area where masked and unmasked areas meet.

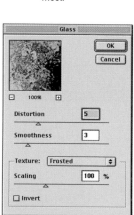

4 Not all filters are suitable for creating edges, but distort-type filters are usually successful. Choose a filter such as Glass. It's helpful to review the effect (and make any changes) in the filter's dialogue box.

5 Apply the filter. The mask will now show the new outline, including the filter effect.

6 Return to normal mode and invert the selection. This makes the new edges active. Press Delete to remove them.

7 The result with white as the background.

8 This was the result with black as the background and a frosted glass filter.

9 The Diffuse Glow filter produces something else again.

Below are two more images produced in exactly the same way, using the indicated filter.

You needn't be restricted to stock filters. Once your border is framed with the Quick Mask, you can paint on, or paint away, any parts of the mask to create your own custom shape, as in the examples below.

Ocean Ripple filter.

1 Above, the edges of the rectangular mask have been softened by using the Airbrush tool.

2 Next, a mid-grey (rather than black or white) was used to paint a transparent mask over the top and bottom of the image.

Extrude filter.

3 The result, right, has soft, flowing edges, with translucent top and bottom borders.

Left, primitive scrollwork gave rise to an informally finished image.

Photographic edges for cheats

The methods described here for creating photographic edges offer almost limitless possibilities. But there are shortcuts. Many of the most popular image editing applications come complete with templates for all manner of edges. Here are just a couple that are similarly conceived to our Quick Mask examples. Images can be pasted into the black area.

If you've got a taste for frames, remember that some applications also feature equally large ranges of ready-made frames into which you can drop your image.

Here is a range of examples, from basic, cropped image frames to more elaborate frames featuring colour and texture. Make sure that any frame you use enhances your image; while some examples are great for party invites, for example, they may not be suitable for framed prints. All of the examples here come from Paintshop Pro and CorelDRAW.

Spatter pattern.

Square Wave pattern.

Above, magnetic numbers make an ideal frame for a child's portrait. Left, an unconventional approach.

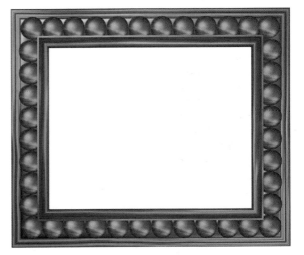

Above, a well-executed, complex arrangement.

Above and left, conventional framing solutions.

Filter effects

Forget about photographic filters – Skylight, UV and polarising or whatever. Digital imaging filters are far more potent and substantially more diverse. Whether you want to hone your photos into works of art, change the tone or turn them into unusual abstract forms, filters – or effects as they are sometimes described – can help.

Filters are often among the first features that newcomers explore. Though there is no doubt that they offer a shortcut to dramatic images, like all power tools they deserve respect. As more than one digital imaging manual says: simply applying a filter is no recipe for a good image. To get results, you need to understand them.

Filter groups

So extensive are the ranges of filters available (many of them offered by image editing packages) that they are best described in categories. Here's an overview, along with some typical images. These categories also provide a convenient way for the creators of image editing software to arrange their filters – even though, apart from the obvious (such as Sharpen and Blur), they are really somewhat arbitrary.

Artistic

'Artistic' filters include those designed to convert your images to drawings and paintings. The effect of those with names such as Watercolour, Impressionist and Palette Knife is reasonably obvious, but this extensive category includes more unusual effects such as Plastic Wrap and Neon Glow. Even the more mundane filters – like Watercolour – offer such a range of controllable effects that the results need not be as simple or blatant as an obvious watercolour painting.

Distort

Filters in this category produce distortions in either two or three dimensions. They can, for example, map your image on to the

Watercolour can simulate the painting technique from which it gets its name, but it can also be used to create somethin с with less obviou с origins.

surface of a sphere, give it a series of ripples or even shear your image about chosen axes. Image distortion, even by the already demanding standards of image editing, requires much computing power; you'll need to dedicate large amounts of memory to processing if you want to avoid long waits.

Plastic Wrap, another Artistic filter, gives a 'vacuum packed' look

Crosshatch gives your image the look of having been painted with a dry brush.

The Glass distort filter produces an impression of viewing through patterned glass.

Though extreme, the Polar Co-ordinates distort filter is useful for creating anamorphic views.

Noise

'Noise' is a somewhat misleading name for a group of filters that both add noise and remove artefacts from images. They can be used to remove small blemishes, such as those caused by dust and scratches.

Atmospheric grain effects can be introduced by the Add Noise filter.

You can use Dust & Scratches and Despeckle filters to clean up dirty scans.

Add Noise-type filters give texture to areas that are over-smooth either through intensive editing or from the use of colour fills.

Pixelate

Pixelate filters clump together pixels – in various distinct ways – and assign a single colour value to each cluster. The image loses in absolute resolution, but often gains a bold graphic quality.

Sketch

Though strictly a subset of the Artistic filters, Sketch filters put a particular emphasis on emulating traditional drawing techniques, with obvious effects such as Charcoal, Crayon and Graphic Pen. Their main difference from Artistic filters is their use of 'foreground' and 'background' colours to build sketched images, rather than original colours. Other representational filters in this category include Note Paper (textured images) and Photocopy. The latter styles the image as if it has been reproduced by a primitive photocopier.

Stylize

Deliberately graphic effects result from Stylize filters. This category includes filters such as Solarize (a digital version of the traditional darkroom technique), as well as the more bizarre Extrude, that makes any image appear as if it has been extruded through a grid. It is fair to say that many of the Stylize effects are very powerful, but to the trained eye, also very obvious. They need to be used with particular care in order to avoid clichés.

Render

A mixed bag, Render filters are used to render textures (cloudscapes are popular) and apply lighting effects. Some filter sets (including Photoshop Elements) add manipulative filters that enable objects to be manipulated in three-dimensional space.

Plug-ins

These, along with the Blur and Sharpen sets already explored, comprise the rump of filter sets, but there are still thousands of others. Many are provided as *plug-ins*, small program modules that plug in to the architecture of the host image editing application. Adobe pioneered the plug-in as a way to expand the capabilities of Photoshop, but most of the major applications now accept Photoshop-compliant plug-ins, and hence can use the almost limitless range available.

Original.

Original.

Colour Halftone screens are simulated with the filter of the same name.

Crystallize (e.g. Facet and Fragment) break the image into fragments that are then coloured according to the average of the fragment's contents.

Mezzotint rebuilds the image as a series of stroked lines.

Pointillized images have a very graphic look.

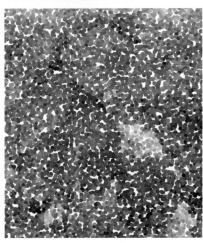

Graphic Pen (used here with blue as the foreground colour) redraws the image with parallel lines similar to that of a Rotring® type pen.

Chalk and Charcoal render your image in these contrasting media.

Though classed a Sketch filter, Chrome gives the impression of a metallic coating.

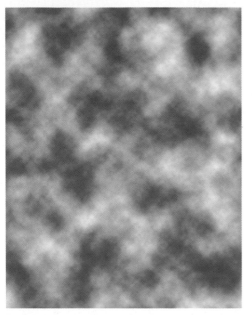

The Clouds filter renders a random skyscape of light fluffy clouds that can be used to replace existing dull skies in your images. Change the foreground and background colours from blue and white and you can get more surreal effects.

Though you would normally try to avoid lens flare, the filter with the same name adds flare to an otherwise clean image. The filter can simulate several lens types: telephoto, wide-angle and zoom.

Lens flare can alter the lighting of a scene. This shot was taken with the sun behind, but the filter gives the impression of shooting into the light.

Original.

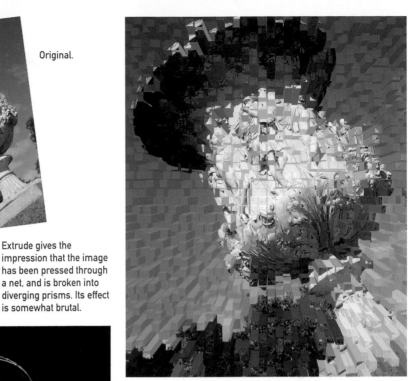

Extrude gives the impression that the image has been pressed through a net, and is broken into diverging prisms. Its effect is somewhat brutal.

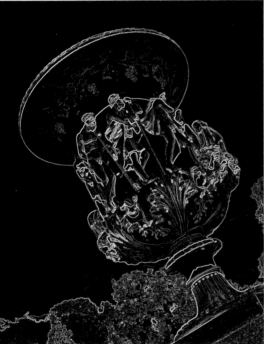

The Glowing Edges filter first identifies sharp edges in the image and then gives them an enhanced glowing appearance based on the actual colour of the subjects. Other areas of the image are coloured black.

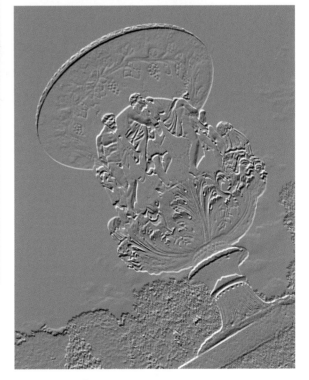

The Emboss filter makes the subject of your image appear to be pressed in low relief into plaster or lincrusta. You can vary the depth of the impression and also the angle at which light appears to strike.

Plug-ins often feature novel interfaces and a number of control parameters. Lightning, from Alien Software's Xenofex, is a particularly effective and controllable filter. Not only can you control the area to which the filter is applied, but you can also control the degree of complexity in the lightning fork, specifying the amount of branching, jaggedness and glow.

The Stain filter, also from Xenofex, is an excellent way of making a new image look aged. The filter makes the main picture area look faded and water-stained, while the edges retain more of the original look. A randomizing feature common to most Xenofex filters ensures that their filter effects are slightly different every time you use them.

Fraxplorer, one of a set of filters comprising Kai's Power Tools, creates 'semi-random' patterns based on fractal principles. Like some other filters from this set, Fraxplorer is more an exploration in colour and pattern than an effect to apply to your images.

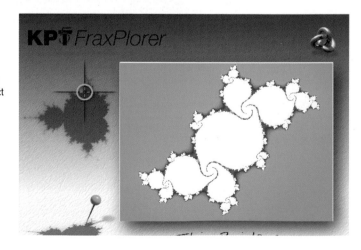

Elements' Filter Browser gives an indication of the appearance of a filtered image.

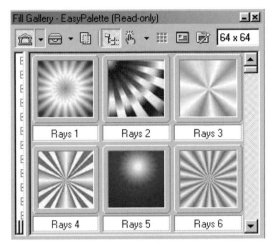

The EasyPalettes in PhotoImpact use pictorial representations for filter effects (and other effects) that can be dragged and dropped on to an image or selection. Like other filter effects, compound effects can be produced by applying a second (or even a third) filter.

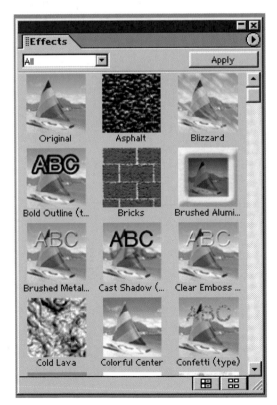

The Effects Browser in Elements illustrates the look of compound filter effects.

Filter preview

Many image editors provide useful filter previews: a set of thumbnail images featuring a typical result of each filter. In Photoshop Elements, a Filter Browser palette is provided (along with one for Effects, Adobe's term for compound filter effects). Other applications have similar features, such as the EasyPalettes option in Ulead's PhotoImpact. Many of these allow you to apply a filter by dragging its thumbnail on to your working image.

Creating your own Old Master painting

Artistic filters are for turning your photos into instant 'works of art'.

1 Prepare your image by making any minor edits. As some of the brush-stroke filters scale their effects by pixel dimensions, ensure that your image is approximately the same size as your final intended output size. If it is too small, brush strokes could be oversized; too large, and the effects will become unrealistically fine.

By giving the layer an Opacity of around 60 percent, some of the detail in the background is revealed.

2 Create a duplicate layer of your image. This allows you to blend layer and background images later to alter the density of any effect applied.

The Cutout filter produces a primitive, paint-by-numbers effect.

3 Apply your filter. Try Rough Pastels and Cross Strokes. The example here was created using Cross Strokes. Use the dialogue box's preview panel to monitor the extent of the brush strokes.

4 Use the Opacity control for the layer to blend the filtered image with the background. In Photoshop, you could alternatively use the Fade Filter command. In this case, you need not create a layer; the Fade command acts on the filtered background.

Sprayed Strokes gives the impression of dragging a brush across the painted canvas.

Dry Brush gives a softer result than Paint Daubs, below.

Paint Daubs uses small, outlined blocks of colour to simulate the action of paint applied by palette knife.

Tip

Use matte or satin finish papers when printing your masterpieces; glossy surfaces betray the non-painted nature of your results.

Better still, check out specialist inkjet printer papers, including those from Lyson and Polaroid. These offer finishes resembling watercolour paper and even canvas.

Don't use real art papers in your inkjet printer (unless certified as suitable). Their fibrous quality gives unpredictable results, and in extreme cases can clog your printer. Replacement or repair can be costly.

If you want to replicate an extensive range of painting and sketching media, applications such as Art Dabbler and Procreate Painter are worth considering.

Painterly effects can also work well with portraits. Take care that the size of the brushstrokes does not reduce the detail in the subjects' faces.

Creating a watercolour

Some filters have only a single operation or a single effect: Sharpen, for example applies a degree of sharpening, but offers no user control of precisely what degree of sharpening is applied.

Others, and in particular the Artistic filters, offer control over many of the parameters that define the filter's effect. Creating a watercolour from a photographic image will show you how.

1 Here's an image suitable for the basis of a painting. You should spend some time choosing your images. Not all filters – or rather their effects – are appropriate for all images.

2 Select the Watercolour filter. A dialogue box like this will open.

3 You can now adjust the Brush Detail, Shadow Intensity and Texture. Brush detail defines the amount of detail shown; with a low level of detail the look is rather like a watercolour painted with a large loose brush. Shadow intensity adds shadow to darker regions; high levels of intensity create dark, moody images. Sliding the Texture control towards a higher value increases the sharpness of the brush detail. Here's our image with low and high values of texture.

4 Which is the correct setting? There is none. Some combinations of settings will be more effective than others, some will be more authentic – but it is up to you to decide which *you* like best. For this image (above) the modest settings shown in the dialogue box on the previous page were used, with each of the three parameters set close to their minimum settings. Of course, when you are working digitally, if the results are not to your liking, you can step backwards and make changes.

Tip

If you are printing on to 'normal' paper, you may find that a normal application of the painterly or artistic effect in question is appropriate. As mentioned earlier, matte paper is to be preferred to glossy. However, if you've taken note of the Tip on the previous spread (and are using simulated watercolour or even canvas-finish paper), you may want a slightly *softer* effect. This avoids the situation where, when printed, the texture of the paper accentuates the effect and makes it appear a little unnatural.

Here are further examples of images
treated with the Watercolour filter.

Top and right, to get a light, fluid
look the original images were
lightened (using the
Brightness/Contrast controls)
before the filter application.

Joining the Impressionists

If the look of a watercolour is a little too formal, why not try the Impressionist look? Impressionist filters work in essentially the same way as Watercolour, but they further dilute the detail in the shots. Photoshop Elements features an Impressionist Brush that, in all practical regards, can be considered a filter *brush*. This brush paints with loose strokes that

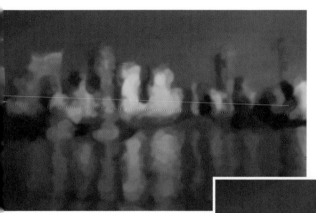

soften the lines and texture of the original image. The result is an image that, true to the ideals of the Impressionists, gives a soft, informal view.

Here, we've taken an original image and applied the Impressionist brush with increasingly fine strokes. The brush size is shown against each image.

Brush size:
25 pixels

Brush size:
10 pixels

Brush size:
3 pixels

Making the effect match the picture

It is important to ensure that the paint brush size is matched to the final size of your picture. Too fine a brush on a large picture can make the detailing seem blurred. Too large an effect on a small image will look more Abstract than Impressionist.

Applying lighting effects

Lighting effects filters offer the chance to alter (with either subtle or obvious effect) the original lighting in your scene. Different lighting sets, for example, enable daylight scenes to be rendered in moonlight, and image subjects to be spotlit. What is more, you'll find that for each lighting effect, there are a number of ways to implement the effect.

Note that most applications feature the lighting types described here, though in some cases the names and the details of how each effect is implemented may be different.

Flashlight

Flashlight is a good example of a single lighting type that can produce different effects. The Flashlight dialogue box offers a number of control parameters, but the important ones are the position and size control (shown here as a thumbnail), and intensity.

The latter gives us the somewhat obvious option of controlling the lighting effect's strength.

Let's give this image a Flashlight look.

1 Set a moderate size (about one-third the width of the image) and position the centre approximately over the subject's head.

2 Apply the filter. An effective flashlight effect is achieved.

3 We can make the effect more intense (but no less authentic) by applying the filter effect again, this time with a slightly larger radius.

We can also use Flashlight (with its default settings) to create a flat-lit scene that appears as if taken via a camera-obscura or even through a telescope.

Blue Omni

This lighting technique can be used in combination with the ambient lighting in the scene – and despite the effect's name, it need not be restricted to blue. (We will use the same technique to create a monochromatic moonlit effect on page 127.)

We can use the effect, for example to change the time of day. This canal side scene (left) was taken at midday. By changing Blue Omni's colour from blue to orange we can make it appear to have been taken towards the end of the day.

5 Here's the same scene with Blue Omni used in it's normal blue state. For added effect we've applied the Lens Flare filter discreetly to suggest the moon.

1 Click on the colour swatch to open the Colour Picker. Choose a rich orange colour.

2 Move the centre of the light circle to the subject of the image (in this case, the bow of the canal boat).

3 Alter the Ambient lighting slider so that the original lighting and new orange lighting are balanced.

4 Click OK. The result gives the appearance of a scene being lit by the setting sun. Though clearly a warm light, the blues and greens in the scene have not been compromised.

Lighting effects

Here is a selection of Lighting Effect options used with their notional default settings.

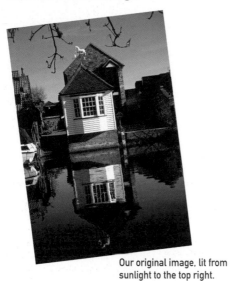

Our original image, lit from sunlight to the top right.

2 o'clock Spotlight gives a tight spotlight directed at the 2 o'clock position.

RGB Lights provides moveable red, green and blue spotlights to illuminate elements of the scene.

Five Lights Down gives a simple stage-lighting effect.

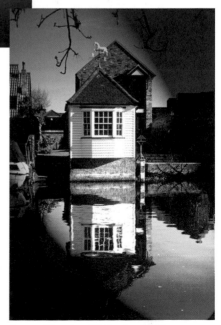

Default lighting provides an adjustable, broad downlight.

Three coloured lights plus white comprise *Circle of Light*, and provide a look rather like garden or Christmas lights strung around the image.

Coloured Spotlight lets the user select any colour for the spotlight beam.

Three positionable spotlights are the some-what obvious lighting for *Triple Spotlight*.

A more diffuse but still directional light source is delivered by *Soft Spotlight*.

Contre-jour

Photographs taken against the light (with the exception of sunsets) are often disappointing. If the camera's light meter assesses the overall light level, your subject – be it a person or a landscape – is reduced to a silhouette. Point the meter away from the subject and the surroundings end up washed out. Some cameras have *backlight compensation* controls. These simply increase the exposure (by a factor of two, sometimes a little more) so that any silhouettes are brightened – no real answer.

1 Start with an assessment of your image. Which parts are correctly exposed? Which are too light? And which are too dark? You may find that, as here, the sky (the predominant light source) has skewed the exposure so that the sky itself is correctly exposed but the main subjects are too dark.

2 You need to select these darker regions and work on them. The simplest way is to select the sky (say using the Magic Wand) and then invert the selection. Brighter areas like skies are often easier to select in such cases than more varied ones.

3 Use the Brightness control to lift the brightness level slightly. This is successful to a point, but the result doesn't blend well with the sky.

This problem is known as 'contre-jour'. One solution is to use spot metering. Some cameras can alter the area of the image from which exposure readings are taken from the entire field of view to a more selective area that may be from one to five percent of the total scene. By selecting Spot Meter you can then take the reading off the subject.

The drawback with this – as with the backlight compensation method – is that it does not change the range of brightness in the scene. By metering of the subject we are likely to render the entire background overexposed and washed out – probably to such a degree that we could not rescue it using any digital darkroom technique.

Using a fill-in flash can often equalize lighting levels to create a more even result;

but assuming you haven't done that, here's how to rescue that contre-jour shot that didn't have the benefit of flash assistance, or that expansive scene that flash couldn't hope to illuminate.

Why contre-jour?

There's nothing mystical about the name – it's French for 'against the 'daylight'. The term distinguishes this lighting type from backlighting, which usually describes a studio lighting technique.

4 Increasing the contrast a modest amount will revive the selection somewhat and remove some of the flatness invoked by the Brightness command. As shadows tend to mute colours, you should also consider increasing the colour saturation.

The result is faithful to the original scene, but allows us to see details more clearly and is better balanced.

Next, try taking the image one step beyond simple lighting corrections. Apply a lighting effect filter (in this case Blue Omni) to give the scene a moonlit appearance. Had you applied this to the original scene, the silhouette and the shading of the house would have been too great, and the effect nowhere near so authentic.

Rediscovering black and white

For most of us, black and white images are something of a Cinderella. While enthusiasts appreciate that some of the most exceptionally compelling photographic images are black and white, the average person rarely gives it a second thought.

But digital imaging has given black and white (a term used here in preference to monochrome – because that, in the digital world, is not necessarily the same) a new lease of life. Not only can you breathe new life into black and white shots, but you can take colour images and create distinctly different black and white images from them.

First, breathing life into real black and white shots. Much of what has already been said about colour photography

applies also to black and white. Above right is a shot that might be typical of those lying ignored in many a family's drawers. Surprisingly (especially considering the very average quality), this is a contemporary image taken on Kodak APS Black and White film (ISO400).

A look at the Levels for this image immediately highlights its shortcomings. The image is completely lacking in tonal

components at either end of the histogram; and these correspond to the blacks and whites that would add punch to this image.

Use the sliders under the histogram to change the tonal distribution. Drag the one on the left to the start of the histogram (this defines your black point), and

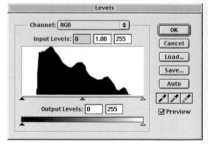

likewise the one on the right to the end of the histogram curve (this defines the white point). Immediately, the image gains some punch (*see* left).

Some fine adjustment to the central slider is now needed to give the shot a final tweak; more a matter of taste than science.

Black and white from colour

Getting a black and white image from a colour shot would seem simple: you could set colour saturation to zero, or use Desaturate. The result would, however, be disappointing. A colour digital image minus

the colour does not give the same result as shooting the same scene using black and white film. Instead, you need to explore colour channels.

A conventional image viewed on screen actually comprises three images, each comprising the red, blue and green components. In effect, your colour image is composed of three black and white images each representing one colour and then combined using an appropriate coloured filter. Each image is, in fact, equivalent to a photo taken on black and white film through a corresponding filter.

The colour image shown here is made up of reds (from the fruit), greens (foliage) and blues (sky). In terms of colour, they create its impact. If you split these into separate colour channels, you get some rather interesting results (below).

So, from a single colour image you have three black and white images of distinctly different character. Which is correct? Impossible to say. All three are distinct, and, it could be argued, equally accurate representations, of the scene; none are correct.

Red Channel: as if taken through a red filter, the sky has been darkened, but the red fruit appear almost white.

Green Channel: the foliage, and to a lesser extent the sky, are lightened in this channel.

Blue Channel: the sky, as you might expect, is now very light, but the red fruit look very dark.

To get a more balanced result, you need to take elements of all three images, using the Channel Mixer. You can mix the three images, in various combinations, to deliver a result that could represent the scene better or, if you wish, to add drama.

In some applications, the Channel Mixer is an Adjustment Layer.

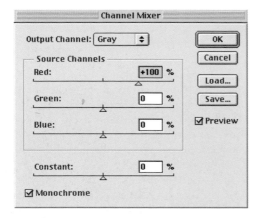

Alter the balance until you have achieved a satisfactory result. It's a good idea not to be too heavy handed with any adjustments. Aim to make the arithmetic sum of the channels add up to 100 percent. Anything substantially more or less than this will have an overall light or dark appearance that suggests either over- or under-exposure. Use the Constant slider to make small compensating adjustments.

In our treatment below, the red channel was supressed a little to avoid overly dark and dominant fruit, boosting the green.

Coloured highlights
Slicing though the traditional demarcation that exists between black and white and colour photography, you can get some fascinating effects by using blend modes in the Channel Mixer. Change the blending mode from default to colour, then select and deselect the Monochrome box. Now, if you move the colour sliders and alter the output channels, you will produce coloured (it would be wrong to call them toned) black and white images. There are two examples on the opposite page. The results can be a little hit and miss, so it is worth recording your settings if you achieve an effect you like and want to recreate it later.

Printing black and white shots
Printing carefully compiled black and white images on printers nominally designed for printing in millions of colours can be problematic. The standard inks and pigments

are in theory capable of recreating subtle greys, but there is always the chance of colour casts.

If you have had experience in handling black and white negatives, you will be familiar with the wide tonal range they are capable of delivering in print. Digital printing, by contrast, can sometimes produce disappointing results with black and white images. Setting your printer to use only the black ink cartridge can often be the answer, but for the best results, consider using inks specially designed for black and white printing. Companies such as Lyson offer cartridges compatible with many printers that replace the three or five coloured inks with blacks and greys.

Consider also, for that extra special image, the option of Duotone or Tritone printing (*see* pages 73–75). Though these are normally used with a second and third coloured ink respectively, their principal use is in extending printing tones from the normal 50 or so levels to 100 or more.

This is the technique that is often used in printing high-quality monochrome art books, where the additional tones created are essential to achieving the degree of quality required.

Monochrome is not black and white

There is a tendency to use the terms 'monochrome' and 'black and white' synonymously. Remember there is a subtle difference. A black and white image is a monochrome image using black and white and shades of grey. Monochrome images can be of any single colour, using only shades of that colour for intermediate tones.

History

The *undo* command is an excellent way of backtracking to your last image edit, and provides a way of testing (and then removing) effects or manipulations. Once upon a time this was the only possible retraction. Any changes made before the last were irrevocably part of the image.

Now, History Palettes, History Brushes and multiple *undo* commands make it easy to step backwards through a project, sometimes up to as many as 100 steps. It's ideal not only for making dynamic modifications but also, if you are new to digital imaging, for exploring features in the knowledge that you can backtrack.

History palette

Every command you make is recorded sequentially in the History palette, up to a user-specified number. Normally this is set at around 20, but can be extended to 100. As each state is stored in memory, it's a good idea to choose a number somewhat less than this maximum to avoid compromising computer performance.

Below, you will see a typical palette. It shows that after the image was opened, a rectangular selection was applied (earliest commands are at the top). Then the *auto levels* and *back light* commands were used. Some editing was then performed using the Airbrush and Clone tools.

If you wish to backtrack to a particular point (say, in this example, before you began using the Clone tool), you can click on the relevant item and your image will be returned to the condition that applied at that stage. You can then either click on subsequent states to view the image in that condition, or start work again from that point. In this case, the subsequent states will be deleted.

1. The aim is to make modifications that will emphasize the wood texture and increase the sense of drama.

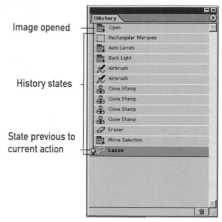

Image opened

History states

State previous to
current action

Photoshop's History palette offers perhaps the most extensive range of options.

History brush

Offered in Photoshop and some other applications, the History Brush lets you selectively brush away any edit states in an image back to a selected state. It could be used, for example, where an image has been heavily modified, but you wish to remove some of the edits from only part of the image. Here's an example:

2 First, the levels have been altered to increase the contrast and darken the image slightly. Note how the History palette acknowledges this change.

3 Selecting the sky first and then the foliage, you can alter (increase) the saturation and lightness to gain bolder colouration.

4 Don't worry if at this stage the colours seem too bright, or even lurid. For example, some of the neutral regions (such as the grey path to the front right of the scene) have become discoloured by over-saturation.

5 Now, with the History brush selected, you can paint over these super-saturated regions and return them to pre-saturation condition. Here you have returned the pathway to that original state, whilst the foliage has been subdued by using the history brush set to 50 percent opacity.

6 Here, on a close-up of the image, the effect of the History brush is obvious. The left-hand side of the scene has been restored to the original state.

Snapshots

The History palette offers a terrific aide-memoire, but if you find it hard to remember precisely what the image *looked like* at a particular state, you need Snapshot.

The Snapshot command enables a temporary copy – or snapshot – of an image in the current history state to be preserved, and to be recalled when the snapshot is clicked on. Any snapshot – or snapshots – you create will be listed sequentially at the top of the History palette, along with a small thumbnail of the image. Note, however, that these are merely temporary copies; when an image is closed – even if you have saved it – all the associated snapshots will be lost.

You can use snapshots for switching between different history states. You might use this option, for example, to assess the impact of different effects (or different applications of the same effect) upon a single image. Take one snapshot before applying, say, a filter and another afterwards. Then click on the 'before' snapshot to return to that state and apply another effect.

Snapshots also provide a useful way of taking large backward steps. If you have applied a great number of steps to an image (for example, if you have repeatedly used the Clone tool or the Airbrush), you may find that you have used so many steps that it is impossible to undo to the previous state. If you have a snapshot of this state, all you have to do is click on the thumbnail to restore the image. On the facing page is a History palette with a snapshot taken at each principal stage.

Cautions

Though the History brush and palette are powerful controls, they come at a cost. As already mentioned, the palette requires substantial memory. If you set it to record 20 steps, then apply the twenty-first, the first entry in the palette will be lost. This is a first-in, first-out system. Also note that changes made at application level (such as preference settings and palette changes) are not recorded as part of the history.

Finally, be warned that some changes
(changes to scale, for example) make it
impossible to use the History brush to
return parts of the image to their condition
prior to that particular change being made.

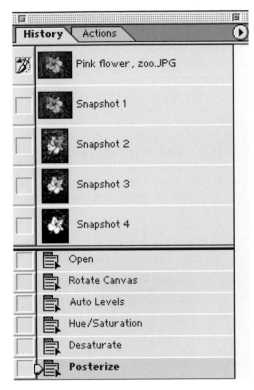

The History palette lets us save snapshots – edit history
states – as often as we wish.

Montage basics

It's all in the layers

Montage – the combining of two or more elements from different photographs – is one of the most powerful and visually impressive of the tools in the digital photographer's arsenal. Whilst the techniques involved are relatively simple, there is much more to good montage than a mastery of the tools themselves.

Producing montages has been made much easier in the last few years with the introduction to most image editing applications of 'layers'. Layers allow you to place elements of a montage on top of each other without affecting any of the underlying pixels, so you can move the elements around at will without committing yourself. Each layer can have any number of transparent pixels, allowing pixels from the layer below to show through.

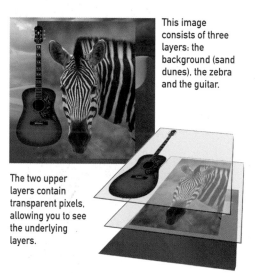

This image consists of three layers: the background (sand dunes), the zebra and the guitar.

The two upper layers contain transparent pixels, allowing you to see the underlying layers.

The transparent areas of a layer are usually shown as a feint checkerboard grid

The power of layers is extended by the ability to alter the opacity and blending mode of each layer.

Photoshop layers palette

Layers are manipulated using the layers palette. From here you can hide layers, select them and change a huge range of variables concerning how they interact.

You can change the order of layers by simply dragging them to a new position.

Getting to know this palette is vital to the effective use and manipulation of Photoshop's powerful layering features.

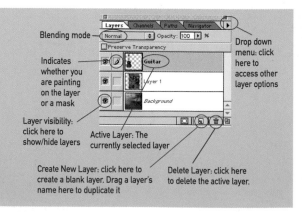

Blending mode

Indicates whether you are painting on the layer or a mask

Layer visibility: click here to show/hide layers

Active Layer: The currently selected layer

Drop down menu: click here to access other layer options

Create New Layer: click here to create a blank layer. Drag a layer's name here to duplicate it

Delete Layer: click here to delete the active layer.

Basic montage technique

One of the most common photo-montage exercises is to change the background of an image. This could consist of adding a new sky to a landscape, or placing a person in a new scene, but the basic aim is the same – to combine two photos into one.

We'll start off with a very simple example, replacing the rather dull background from the portrait below with something a little brighter.

3 Use a small brush to clean up the edges of the selection as much as possible. Use black paint to add to the mask (i.e. remove areas of the selection), and white paint to remove parts of the mask (extend the selection). When you are ready, turn the mask back into a selection (in Photoshop, just press *Q* again; in other applications, turn off the *paint on mask* option).

4 We now need to put our cut-out subjects on to their new background. There are several ways to do this, depending on the application you are using. Most applications allow you simply to open both pictures and drag from one to the other (using the Move tool). Dragging one image to another in this way will create a new layer in the target image containing the pixels from the image you are dragging. If you have a live selection (as we have here), the new layer will only contain the pixels inside the selection.

1 Our first job is to cut out our subjects. The secret to seamless montages lies in the edges; any stray pixels from the old background – known as 'fringing' – will make for a glaringly unrealistic composite. Above, we've used Photoshop's Magnetic Lasso to trace the outline. The Magnetic Lasso automatically detects edges, and in situations like this one, where the background has too much detail to use the Magic Wand, it's a great start point.

2 Applications such as Photoshop allow you to turn the 'marching ants' selection into a mask overlay that can be edited using paint tools. This is a great way to clean up the edges of your selection. In Photoshop, the mask appears by default as a ruby red overlay, and is accessed via the *edit in quick mask* mode command (simply press *Q*).

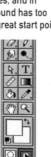

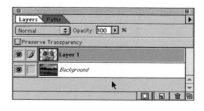

5 Above is the Layers palette for our target image, showing the original photo (Background layer) and the new layer (Layer 1) floating above it. If the new layer is the wrong size, use the Transform tools (in Photoshop, found under the Edit>Transform menu) and stretch it to size.

6 You can now do any final tweaks necessary on the edges of Layer 1. Use the Eraser tool with a small brush size to remove any stray pixels. For the final image (below), we adjusted the levels of each layer to match colour and brightness, and applied a Gaussian Blur to the background layer.

Tip

When painting on masks or erasing stray pixels, make sure you use the right brush: soft brushes for soft edges and hard brushes for hard edges. Photoshop's special textured brushes can be very useful for difficult-to-mask regions, such as hair or foliage.

Using layer masks

The method described on the preceding pages is perfectly good for most montages, but what happens if later on you decide to make slight changes in the cut-out of your placed elements? Using layers makes removing pixels from each element easy, but if you want to add extra detail from the original scene, you need to go back and repeat the whole process of cutting out and placing the element. This can easily happen if you place an element and then accidentally erase too much of its layer – or if the cut-out is simply wrong in the first place. Fortunately, there is a less 'destructive' way of masking a layer than blithely deleting pixels.

We'll use a simple example – putting this old Dakota into flight (using a shot taken, incidentally, from the same plane).

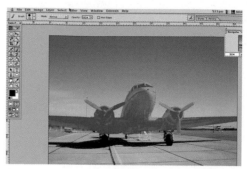

2 A quick clean-up with the Quick Mask sorts out any areas the Magnetic Lasso has missed. Exit Quick Mask mode, and the cut-out is complete.

3 We now need to add a 'layer mask' based on our selection. A layer mask is a special greyscale mask that hides areas of a layer and can be edited independently. With your selection active, simply click on the Add a Mask icon at the bottom of the layers palette.

You will immediately see your cut-out subject on a transparent background. (Note that Photoshop won't let you apply a layer mask to the Background layer. To convert the background to a 'normal' layer, simply double-click on it in the layers palette, then click on OK.)

1 The first job – as previously – is to isolate the plane from its background. We've used the Magnetic Lasso again to trace the edge of the plane (without its landing gear).

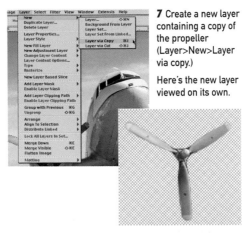

7 Create a new layer containing a copy of the propeller (Layer>New>Layer via copy.)

Here's the new layer viewed on its own.

4 Open your target image (the sky) and drag the layer – that is, its layer mask – from the plane image (simply click on the layer in the layers palette and drag it onto the window containing the sky). You may want to scale or rotate the layer containing the new element – if so, now is the time to do it (use edit>transform>free transform to scale and rotate in one go).

5 If the edges of the cut-out plane need attention, click on the layer mask icon in the layers palette. Use the paintbrush with black or white paint to extend or reduce the

area covered by the mask. Painting on the mask with black hide more pixels from the layer containing the plane, white shows more pixels. You may find it easier to work if you temporarily hide the background layer.

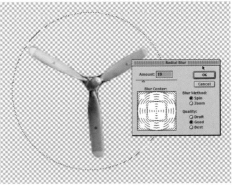

8 Draw a circular selection around the propeller in the new layer and choose the Radial Blur filter (under the Filter>Blur menu). Using the Spin setting, choose an 'amount' of 15–30. This should result in some pretty convincing motion blur (below). You now need to repeat the whole process for the other propeller.

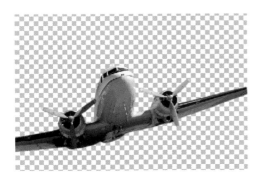

6 Now to add a touch of realism. The propellers should at least appear to be moving if this plane is to look like it is actually flying. Use the Magic Wand or Magnetic Lasso to select one of the propellers. If necessary, clean up the selection using the Quick Mask.

Tip

You can, if you wish, discard the layer mask by dragging it to the 'trash' icon on the layers palette. If you say 'yes' to applying the mask, the hidden pixels will be permanently deleted.

9 Go back to the layer containing the aeroplane, and extend the layer mask to remove the areas of the propeller that extend beyond the engine itself. Viewing the two layers together (the plane and the blurred copy of the prop) gives a pretty realistic representation of rotating blades caught by a relatively high shutter speed.

10 The final image, after each layer had been adjusted for brightness, contrast and sharpness.

11 A further experiment, in which the Lens Flare filter has been applied to the background layer to give the impression of the sun being behind the plane.

Soft edges

So far, we've only looked at cutting out subjects with relatively hard edges. Things get a little more complicated when you need to blend in subjects with soft, indistinct or blurred edges. As an example, we'll make a composite of the two photos below. Note that to make things easier, I've chosen a new background similar in tone to the original.

1 As usual, the first step is to create the selection. With soft edges, most of the standard selection tools struggle, so you often end up doing a lot of the work 'manually'. In this case we used Photoshop's Select>Colour Range command to select all the green areas of the image. We then inverted the selection and smoothed it (Select> Inverse; Select>Modify>Smooth).

2 Some work needs to be done on the selection created in step 1 to take into account the blurred edges. As a first step convert your selection into a Quick Mask and use a soft paintbrush to match the mask to the subject. Remember that as well as adding to the mask with black paint and removing pixels with white paint, you can use shades of grey to create semi-transparent areas.

After tweaking the mask for a while, this is what we ended up with. Note that the blurred parts of the cat are covered by grey areas of the mask.

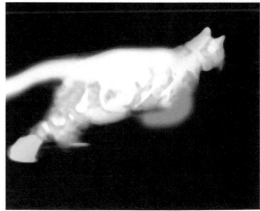

4 Clean up the edges of the cat layer if necessary and the montage is complete.

3 Drag the cat image on to the new background as a new layer; see pages 138–139 for how to do this. Here, we've used the method described there to copy only the pixels inside the selection, but you may decide to add a layer mask to the cat image, as described on pages 140–143.

5 To lend realism, we added a motion blur to the new background and painted a shadow under the cat using the dodge tool.

Flights of fantasy

S o far we've only looked at creating 'realistic' montages – effectively, just placing single elements on to a new background. Once you have mastered the basic tools, you can really let your imagination run wild. We'll start with a relatively simple example; convincingly putting this swimmer into the teacup

4 The mask is a bit too regular to look convincing. To edit the shape click on the mask icon in the layers palette.

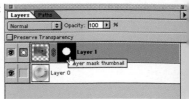

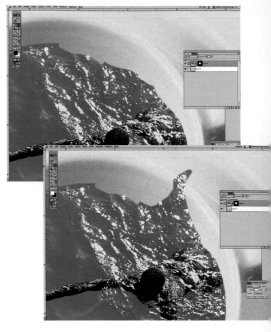

1 Start by opening both images and dragging the swimmer on to the teacup. Scale the new layer if necessary so it just covers the entire cup.

2 Temporarily hide the upper (swimmer) layer and create a selection inside the rim of the cup. I used an elliptical marquee and distorted it using the Select>Transform selection command until it fitted perfectly.

5 Again, use black paint to extend the mask (hide more pixels) and white paint to reduce the masked area. Use a hard edged paint brush to give the water's edge a more natural appearance.

3 With the selection still active, click on the little eye next to the upper (hidden) layer in the layers palette. Make this the active layer by clicking once on its name. You can now create a layer mask for this layer using the selection created in step 2.

6 As the teacup is on a boring white background I decided to add a new one. The first step was to turn the background layer into a 'normal' layer by double clicking on it. Simply select the entire background with the magic wand and press the delete key.

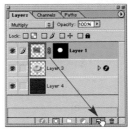

9 To bring back the highlights (which would not be transparent) first duplicate the layer containing the swimmer (the mask will also be duplicated). To duplicate the layer, drag it to the new layer icon on the layers palette.

10 Change the blending mode of the new (duplicate) layer to screen. This will lighten the

entire layer. We only want the highlights, so we need to play with the Layer Options. In Photoshop 5.5 you'll find this listed under the Layers menu, Photoshop 6 puts it in with the Blending Options under the Layer Style menu. In either case you can bring it up by double-clicking on the layer's name in the Layers Palette.

7 You can now add the new background as a separate layer at the bottom of the stack. I've used a texture file from a clipart collection that has been darkened towards the top using a gradient in soft light mode. To complete the effect add a drop shadow to the cup layer (using the Layer Styles menu).

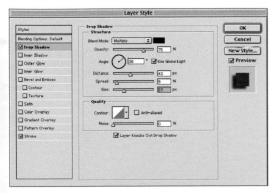

11 The layer blending options include a section called 'blend if'. From here you can define areas of transparency based on the colour of the pixels in the layer and those beneath it. By dragging the black arrows under the 'This Layer' scale to the right we can restrict the visible pixels in the layer to the very brightest (the highlights). The position of the black arrow defines the cut-off point.

12 To prevent an abrupt cut-off point you can define a range of values, giving a smoother blend. Simply hold down the 'alt' key as you click and drag to split the arrow into two. The cut-off will now be a smooth gradient between the two points.

8 The final stage in this montage is to add a little translucency to the water, so we can see the bottom of the cup. Change the blend mode of the layer containing the swimmer/water to Multiply. Note that although this has given us the correct level of translucency, we have also lost the bright white highlights on the water.

13 The finished image

Quick tips for great montages

C ombine all the techniques described on the previous pages for complex montages. This example uses layer masks, blurred copies of layers, drop shadows and 'blend if' changes

To create a quick layer mask use the 'Paste Into' command (under the Edit menu in most applications).

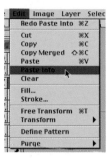

Layer duplicated and motion blur added to lower copy

'Blend if' used to put behind cloud

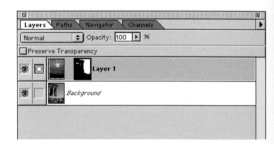

In this example, to put in a new sky we would first select the old sky area (I used the Magic Wand).

Next open your new sky, select all and choose copy (Edit>Copy).

Go back to the original picture (with the selection still active) and choose File>Paste Into ...

... and hey presto, a new layer is created containing the sky you copied complete with a layer mask based on the selection made in step 1.

Use shading (such as cast shadows) to create a more convincing montage. It also always helps to use subjects that have similar backgrounds and lighting.

Layer mask used to put fingers behind cloud

Drop shadow added

To add motion to a cut-out element, make a duplicate of the layer and blur that. You can then mask either or both layers to keep some parts sharp.

Montages always work better when the elements used make sense together, meaning tone, texture and lighting need to match. Adjust the colour of each layer individually to ensure consistency.

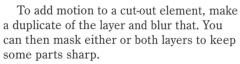

Montage tips

• Think about texture. If the elements for your montage come from different sources – especially if some were shot on film – they may have completely different textures (usually in the form of film grain). This can also happen if your source images are JPEGs and show different levels of compression artefacts. In these cases you may need to add some noise to all layers to 'even out' the texture.

• Think about light and light sources. If you combine more than one object into a montage, you may need to add some shading so that all the elements appear to be lit from the same light source. The dodge and burn tools can be useful in these cases.

• Think about perspective. Always try to use photos shot from roughly the same angle and using a similar lens (i.e. wide or telephoto). Elements with widely differing perspectives will just look 'stuck on'.

• Plan ahead. All the best montages use photographs shot specially for the purpose. This allows you to control lighting and ensure everything fits together perfectly. Sketch out your composition on paper before shooting and take lots of shots from slightly different angles.

• Think about scale. It is very difficult to produce a convincing montage where the scale of certain elements is grossly exaggerated. See any number of 1950s B-Movies about giant ants for a graphic illustration of this point.

• Make life easy. If you are photographing someone especially to put them on a new background, make life easier by using a plain background that contrasts with their hair (one of the most difficult things to mask effectively). A white background can be removed quickly using the *blend if* controls, solid single-colour backgrounds can often be quickly removed using the select>colour range command or even the Magic Mand.

• Save your layers. Even when you think you have finished a montage it makes good sense to save a copy with all the layers (and any layer masks) intact. Should you ever need – or want – to go back and make changes, you will be able to.

• Avoid crude tools such as the smudger, and don't use feathered selections on hard-edged objects to save time. Both will produce unnatural results.

Fantasy images and fun portraits

oving heads or faces from one body to another was one of the earliest – and most dubious – uses of digital software. But this technique is not only about creating compromising situations: it is about (almost) endless innocent fun.

As you become more practised at image manipulation, you'll find that you can create these fantasy images from scratch. Meanwhile, most applications feature some type of montage tool for creating this type of image. Here, ArcSoft's PhotoFantasy™, a neat, self contained package available for Macintosh or PC, has been used.

As with ArcSoft's's PhotoMontage application, PhotoFantasy comes complete with images on which to experiment.

Fantasy image tips

- Once familiar with the processes, you can create your own fantasy backgrounds, using a masking tool to isolate the area of the scene you want replaced.
- As with all montage work, you get a convincing result provided that the new image element appears to be part of the original scene. This means not only correct colour balance, but size. There must also be a credible relationship between the subject's direction of gaze, the camera angle and the background.

1 Begin by choosing a fantasy background. Here is a scene – including a body – on to which you can transpose a head or face, or multiple characters.

2 Here's a selection of the options available, from the believable through to the truly fantastic. Note how the face, or faces, that can be replaced are indicated by a masking colour.

3 A double cut-out makes an amusing experiment.

4 When you select your replacement face, the image appears in the previously masked area. It's unlikely that the fantasy image and your image will be to the same scale, so provision is made to enlarge or reduce it.

5 Similarly, the images may have different colour casts. You can make corrections simply to ensure that they are similar.

6 You can now add this second person to the scene.

7 Again, you need to rescale in order to make the fit convincing.

8 After adjustment to both colour and scale, the fantasy is finished.

Caricatures

Creating caricatures has proven so popular that there is now a package dedicated to just that: SuperGoo (from ScanSoft) provides all the tools you need to warp, twist and distort the faces of family and friends. And it throws in hairstyles, spectacles, hats and even 'new' facial features.

SuperGoo also boasts a very fluid interface (this is the Mac version, but the PC one is identical) that makes the product especially easy and fun to use – whatever your age.

2 Basic face given new hair and a hat.

3 With a single click you can turn the features from male to female – and back again.

1 Add simple effects: above is a ripple and right the face has been turned into a fractal pattern.

4 Adding spectacles....

5 ... and then partly knocking them off

Caricature tip

If you don't have SuperGoo, the Mesh Warp feature in most image editing applications (it's called Liquify in Photoshop) can be used to achieve many of the distortions possible in SuperGoo.

6 ...enlarged facial features...

7 ... then shrunk.

Phototapestries

Once the preserve of ad agencies and the jigsaw puzzle creators, Phototapestries (called PhotoMontage™ by ArcSoft in its products, and photomosaics elsewhere) creates intriguing artwork from your images. The original image is broken down into a grid of very small cells. Then a tiny image thumbnail replaces the content of each cell, whose colour and tone match that of the original content. The result is an image that from a distance appears pixellated, but only on close inspection proves to be something more.

Creating these effects is simple thanks to applications such as MGI's PhotoSuite and ArcSoft's PhotoMontage.

This sequence uses PhotoMontage.

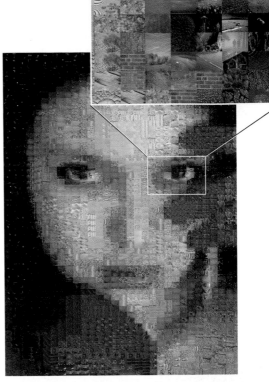

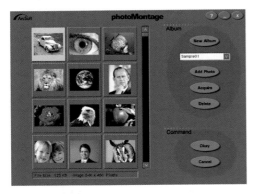

1 Choose your image. The effect works best on simple, bold images. Don't use cluttered landscapes, street scenes or groups of people, for example: they tend to lose too much detail when the thumbnails are applied.

2 This close-cropped portrait is ideal. Both Photosuite and ArcSoft offer a range of sample images on which to practise.

3 Press the Build Montage button.

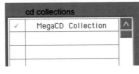

4 Select the image thumbnail collection to be used to reconstruct your image. Again, sample galleries are supplied so that you can begin compiling a phototapestry straight away.

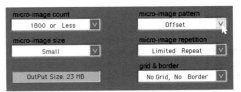

5 Choose the number (and size) of thumbnails required. Smaller thumbnails preserve more of the structure of the original image, but take longer to compile. You can also select the image pattern (aligned on a grid, or offset, like a brick wall). Note, too, that you can set the frequency of image repeat: depending on the number of thumbnails in your gallery, and the number required to build the phototapestry, you can set this to Never, Rarely or Often.

6 Now build the montage. The process is fully automated, but will take several minutes. You can monitor progress on screen.

See the next two pages for more phototapestries.

155

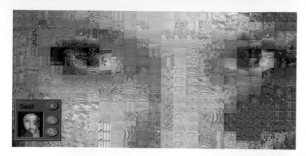

More phototapestries

Note how, using the portrait of the girl (above and left) the number of thumbnails used has a dramatic effect upon the clarity and resolution of the image. Always assess the quality of the final image against the physical size to which it is to be reproduced.

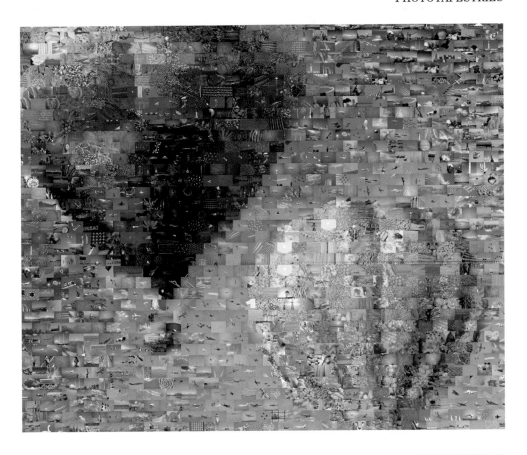

Phototapestry tips

- You can use your own image collections for the thumbnails, or even organize images into separate galleries for application to appropriate image types.

- To make the phototapestry more meaningful, you can create custom thumbnail galleries. For example, for a portrait of a teenager you could use a collection of thumbnails of that person taken when younger.

- PhotoMontage lets you turn the final image into a game by hiding a Golden Key amongst the thumbnails. Recipients have to find it. The same application also allows you to add your signature, in digital form, to the image.

- Additional features, launched from the application, offer such options as acquiring additional thumbnail galleries or poster-sized prints.

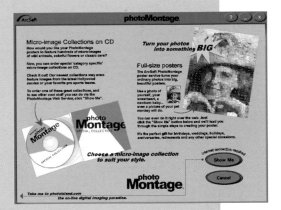

Sabattier effects

In the world of conventional photography, Sabattier refers not to kitchen knives, but to one of the earliest photographic special effects

Creating a Sabattier effect image in an old-fashioned darkroom involves exposing a partially developed print to light. The normal tones reverse as a result of changes in sensitivity from the original exposure. The final effect, as its originator Armand Sabattier described it, is pseudo-solarisation. The difficulty with the Sabattier effect is getting the right balance between the original exposure and mid-development exposure. Even duplicating an otherwise technically sound image is rarely successful.

This makes the Sabattier effect an ideal candidate for the modern digital darkroom. Digital imaging enables you to make controlled, repeatable images, and to extend or diminish the effect easily.

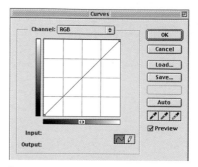

1 Open the Curves dialogue box. The normal appearance of the Curves line is a straight diagonal.

Sabattier tips

The Sabattier effect is, by its nature, imprecise, so there is no right or wrong result. If you are happy with your result, stick with it, and ignore what purists might say.

A useful shortcut to achieve these colour and tone inversions is to use the Solarisation command. Though the effect is slightly different, and often gives more muted colours than with Sabattier, solarisation achieves consistent results instantly.

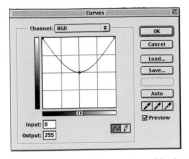

2 Alter the line by clicking on the mid point to fix it; then drag the start point to the top-left.

3 Those parts normally represented by the upper part of the curve are reproduced authentically; the tonal values of the remainder are inverted.

The very obvious and strange results from the Sabattier technique do limit the type of subject on which it can work. Unless uncomfortable results are actually wanted, you'd best avoid appyling the technique to portraits. For your first attempt, choose a simple landscape containing bold shapes – such as the beach scene below.

SABATTIER EFFECTS

4 The image on the previous page is a simple Sabattier. By making subtle changes to the basic shape of the curve, colours and tones can be further altered. Introducing a second dip to the left of the main curve produces the image to the right.

A second dip to the right gives slightly higher colour saturation, below.

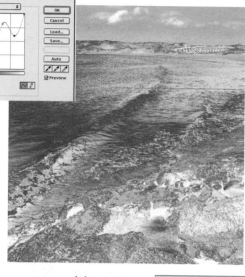

A deeper principal dip creates a much more extreme effect, right.

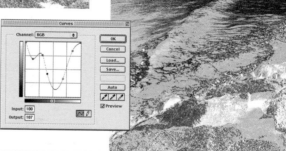

Left, the image with the Solarise effect applied. It is clear that neither Solarise or Sabattier effects are in any way natural and it is easy for the results to be 'uncomfortable' for the viewer. So it is important to have a purpose in mind when applying these effects. Maybe it is to achieve a deliberate unworldly effect?

The Sabattier effect also works with monochrome images. Here, the simple curve described on page 159 has been applied. Note the fine white lines around the edges of some elements of the image. These are the so-called Mackie Lines. The term 'pseudo solarisation' is particularly apt for black and white images where the bright areas are often reversed, as shown here, to become dark.

Powerful panoramas

Panoramic cameras tend to be very specialized, commanding prices beyond the reach of anyone but the well-off devotee.

However, with digital software you can make convincing panoramas just by joining photographs. First, take the shots to be joined. It's straightforward:

- Ensure that your camera is mounted level – preferably on a tripod.

- Select a standard or short telephoto lens – the distortion inherent in wide-angle lenses is unhelpful.

- Make your exposures from left to right, ensuring that each overlaps the one before by around 30 percent.

- Use your camera in the landscape or portrait (upright) position. In landscape you will need fewer images to complete the panorama but that panorama will have less height; portrait panoramas will give greater height but will require around 60 percent more images.

- For absolute precision, a pan and tilt tripod is useful.

Panorama tips

- You may need to make some extra edits to remove any remaining artefacts thrown up, particularly in areas of continuous colour, such as the sky.
- Be extra liberal with overlaps when using wide angle lenses: these introduce distortion that is best countered by increasing the overlap.

3 Create a preview panorama. This stitches the images together at low resolution, so you can preview the joins.

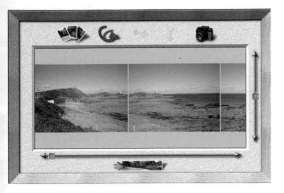

1 Load the images into the software in left to right order – the order in which they will be joined.

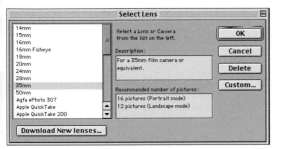

4 If the images have not been precisely stitched together, you can manually fine-tune the joins.

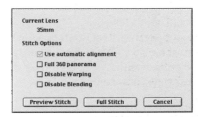

2 Select the focal length (or equivalent) of the lens used – this is to ensure that perspective is maintained.

5 Create the full panorama. If you are using PhotoVista, remember to un-check the 360- degree box unless you have photographed a full 360-degree panorama.

6 Save your image.

The set of images above left follows these criteria exactly. They were shot on a pan and tilt tripod calibrated in degrees, and fitted with a spirit level.

Some applications – for example Photoshop Elements and MGI's Photosuite – have panoramic functions built in.

PhotoVista, also from MGI, is a useful alternative – it is designed solely for the purpose of creating panoramas.

Composite images such as panoramas can have remarkably high overall resolution that is equal to the sum of that of their constituent elements.

More joined images

Panoramic software isn't just for creating sweeping vistas. With a little cunning, it can be used to create vertical views and to produce super-wide-angle shots.

Just as there are times when a scene is simply too wide to record with a single shot, there will be also times when you need extra height. You might, for example, want to photograph the stained glass and roof of a big church, or the full height of a skyscraper, from a vantage point close by.

To produce a vertical panorama, follow the rules for a conventional panorama, with the obvious modification of vertically aligning the exposures, rather than horizontally.

A simple vertical panorama:

3 Because panoramic software doesn't allow vertical panoramas, you have to build your view on its side. Load your images sequentially, starting with the bottom image, with each turned through 90 degrees, so that the bottom of the image is to the left.

4 Build the panorama, right. If your shots are of, say, a tall building, perspective effects may make the automatic picture stitching a little more difficult. If so, be prepared to make manual adjustments.

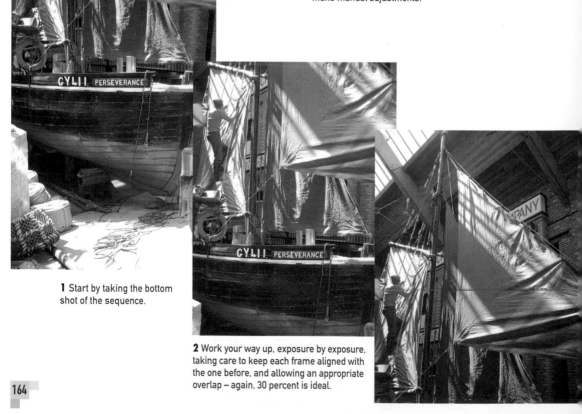

1 Start by taking the bottom shot of the sequence.

2 Work your way up, exposure by exposure, taking care to keep each frame aligned with the one before, and allowing an appropriate overlap – again, 30 percent is ideal.

Tip

For architectural shots (especially interiors), accurate alignment is critical. A tripod with pan and tilt head (rather than ball and socket) is ideal for getting perfect vertical alignment.

Confined spaces

Shooting the street scene below would have been difficult using a single shot: the narrowness of the street would require a very wide angle lens (with consequent distortion of the image) or a plate camera with adjustable lens and film planes. Instead, three conventional wide angle images have been combined.

Left, the standard 35mm lens view. Below, a combination of three images combined to give minimal distortion.

1 Assess your scene. Take your first shot to define the top left hand corner.

2 Move the camera to the right and (observing the overlap rule) take a second shot. The top right hand corner of this shot will define the top right hand corner of the finished image.

Quilting

There is no reason to restrict image joining to linear arrangements. You can also work in two directions, joining images both side by side and above and below. to create a single image. This is known as quilting.

You could create a quilt by joining adjacent panoramas, but some software, including PhotoSuite, lets you build them directly. Here's how to make a super-wide image from four quilted images:

Note how some of the figures in this example have moved between the shots, resulting in a somewhat weird result. Avoiding figures, if possible, to prevent such discontinuities.

And if you don't have a quilting function ...

If your image editing application doesn't allow quilting, you can achieve much the same result in the following way:

1 Prepare to take a matrix of four or nine images in the way shown in the illustrations here. If you are using an SLR camera, use a lens that introduces as little distortion as possible. Rather than using a very wide angle lens, for example, choose a 35mm or even a standard lens and take a larger number of shots.

3 Repeat the process for the bottom left and bottom right hand corners, above and above right.

4 The images can then be combined in exactly the same way as with a conventional panorama.

2 Take the shots, starting from the top left and working horizontally.

3 Arrange the photos in pairs or triplets comprising each row.

4 Use conventional panoramic software to stitch these shots together to produce 'mini-panoramas'.

5 Now stitch the two (or three, if you had nine original images) panoramas together, treating each as an individual image.

The quality of the results will very much depend on the lenses used for taking the shots. Often, you will get an authentic wide-angle effect that, like the quilted example here, would be extremely difficult to take in a single shot. On other occasions, you can get gross distortion of the kind often associated with fisheye lenses. Although distortion like this may be inappropriate for some subjects, it can often have a strong pictorial value.

Slide shows

The very idea is a turn-off for those (perhaps most of us) who've sat through too many 35mm slides of someone else's holiday adventures, accompanied by not-so-funny jokes. Digital slide shows are something else entirely: Imaging software can turn a 'digital photo album' into a dynamic presentations bought alive by captions, titles and sound effects. A great way of sharing your best images and fondest memories – without hassle.

Slide show tips

Don't go overboard on the transitions and sound effects. Simple fades will focus attention on your images, while often the best accompanying sound is silence.

Select a transition between slides. You can have a simple fade, or any one of dozens of others.

Add sound effects if you wish. There's a range of effects supplied that include

With simple software you can import and arrange your images in sequence; create interesting transitions between images and even export your result to CD – to share with friends and family – or export to the web – to share with the world.

Above and right, Kai's Power Show, an inexpensive slide show application, has been used to make a simple show.

Adding images to a show is simple. Select the directory containing the images, and they are automatically added to the desktop. Then either drag and drop them on to the timeline (along the base, as seen above) or allow the application to add them all. You can then rearrange their position in your own time.

Applications such as Kai's Power Show are designed purely for image-based slide shows and multimedia presentations. It gives you extensive options for layouts and sequencing and you can add your own narration or music to enhance the performance.

musical background through to smashing glass and thunderclap noises.

If you want to send it to a friend, copy it to a CD (the CD will, in the case of Power Show, also include a Power Show player – there's no need for the recipient to own the full application). You can even post the show in html format so that it can be viewed on the web.

Greetings cards

Many applications provide greeting card templates and useful clip-art embellishments. Just follow the step-by-step instructions. But it's also easy to make cards without specific prompts.

This birthday party invitation has a climbing theme, but you can create equally effective cards around any theme you care to choose.

To complete the card, you need some wording and, if you plan to print the card out in folded form, you'll need to adjust the position on the page. It helps to make the text stand out if you add a layer effect such as a drop shadow or outer glow. Here, outer glow has been used along with the Stroke command that gives a fine contrast line around the edge of the text.

1 For the main image, the birthday boy was asked to climb a low (and safe) climbing frame in a local park.

Greeting card tips

- Use paper with a printable surface on both sides if you want to create double-sided cards. Some papers are watermarked or printed on the back.
- Use the techniques described earlier to give your images a border or decorative edge prior to printing.
- Fantasy images (page 152) make ideal subjects for party invitations.

2 To give a more ambitious background, use the selection tools to cut away the existing one. You could use conventional selection tools, a quick mask or even a specialized tool such as Photoshop's Extract (continued overleaf).

3 Now you need a convincing background – preferably one that's not too hard to find. You could have used an image scanned from a magazine, or an image from your archive. But here, a small rock was photographed using the digital camera's macro setting in close up. It was also sharpened using the Unsharp Mask filter in order to make it look extra craggy.

4 Combine the shots and adjust the position until it looks convincing.

Personalized calendars

Calendars featuring personalized images can be created in much the same way as greetings cards. Again, many applications feature templates for calendars, though most offer only a restricted number of years on the presumption that you will have upgraded the software before the final year. Some software companies post updated templates on their websites.

This example comes from Photo Soap 2.

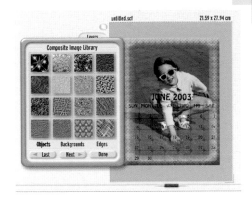

3 To maximize the overlay's clarity (and improve the pictorial qualities of the calendar page) give the image a feathered or decorative edge. In Photo Soap, you can drag and drop any one of a selection of borders.

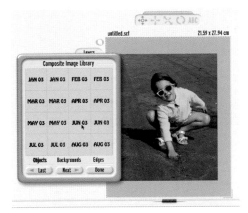

1 Open your image and manipulate it in the way you want. As most calendar templates are overlays, it helps if your image has an area over which this overlay can be placed. Select the year or month to be applied to your image.

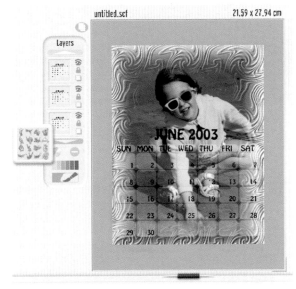

4 You might like to complete your calendar page with some clip art decoration.

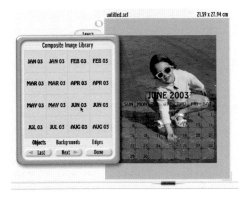

2 Drag and drop the overlay to the image. You can use the adjustment tools to alter the scale of the overlay so that it fits the image.

Blending modes

Called Merge Modes in Corel's Photo-Paint, blending mode options appear frequently in palettes and dialogue boxes of most imaging software. The facility determines how the pixels in an image background (the base layer) interact with those of the layer above (often called the paint layer).

Following this book you've already used blending modes: for example, the Color mode (page 72) used one to apply transparent paint when adding colour a black-and-white image.

It's obvious how most blending modes will work out. For example, Dissolve features the paint layer dissolving into the background layer. In Hue, Luminosity and Color, only the hue, luminosity and colour

Dissolve.

Left, the original, background image.

Below, the image layer (paint layer),

of the paint layer are applied to the background.

Blending mode results can be unpredictable, so it always makes sense to experiment before committing them to your image.

Here two images, a background of a yellow lily and a paint layer of a coin, have been blended. The coin has been saved in one layer (i.e. its surroundings are transparent), then blending modes applied. The results on this page and the next four are typical. Remember that blending modes can be faded from 0 to 100 per cent and that results vary according to setting.

Multiply.

Overlay.

Screen.

Soft Light.

Hard Light.

Color Dodge.

Color Burn.

Darken.

Lighten.

Difference.

Exclusion.

Hue.

Saturation.

Color.

Luminosity.

Working with blending modes

It's not just newcomers to digital imaging who get baffled by blending modes, but they're worth mastering because they can achieve effects that are hard to emulate otherwise. Here are a couple of examples. (Note that the Colour mode is covered on page 72 under hand colouring.)

Building density with the Multiply Blending mode

When you have an image that is very light, or faded, either through overexposure, or from age, the obvious response is to adjust the brightness (and perhaps the contrast) controls in order to restore a broader contrast and tonal range. Instead, consider using the Multiply Blending Mode.

Multiply's basic effect is to sandwich one image with another, in much the same way as, in conventional photography, you might sandwich two transparencies together to create a montage. In such cases, the montage is always darker than the original transparencies.

In digital imaging, your results should be free of the odd effects of combining film bases of different colour.

3 In the Layers palette, change the blend mode from Normal to Multiply.

4 After applying the Multiply blend mode, the image darkens. Also, on close inspection, detail too pale to be visible in the original reappears. This new visual information is *real*.

1 Above, the original overexposed image.

2 Create a new duplicate layer, based on this image. The resulting composite will look no different at this stage.

5 If the image is still a little light, you could repeat the process. Or, at this stage, it would be appropriate to fine tune the Brightness/Contrast commands. With a subtle adjustment, you can create an image that is probably, in this case, as good as the original.

Modifying contrast using Hard and Soft Light

In the image below, the damage is not so much due to fading or over exposure, but to a dramatic loss of contrast. Although this could be down to poor processing, printing or storage of the original, it is more often the result simply of ageing. In this particular example, poor processing is probably the culprit.

3 After the Blend Mode is applied, the contrast improves and, as a useful by-product, the colours are improved, as well.

1 Open the image. Note that the colours are obvious, but somewhat subdued.

Using the Soft Light blending mode gives a similar, but more gentle, increase in contrast. See page 174.

2 As in the previous example, create a duplicate layer. Change the Blend Mode from Normal to Hard Light.

4 In this case, the new image is an improvement, but could still be better. Increasing the contrast (using the Brightness/Contrast command) gives an even better result. Note that using this command earlier would have given a poorer tonal range.

Creating custom effects

Using effects filters on your images can transform the mundane into the truly spectacular. But beware: often, the simple application of a filter can betray itself all too easily. But with a little extra effort, you can modify the action of simple filters in a subtle way and create effects that are far more original, yet no less compelling. Here are two examples.

3 Apply the *Find Edges* filter to the new layer (Find Edges is called *Edges* in some applications). The image takes on a somewhat abstract appearance, above.

Linocut prints

Creating a print-effect from an image is difficult using the conventional effects filter sets, but this method creates an effect that simulates a linocut print.

1 Open your original image. The result will be improved if the contrast and colour saturation is increased very slightly.

2 Create a second layer that is a copy of the original image.

4 Now select the white parts of the image (this can be done using the Colour Range command, or by using the Magic Wand to select one region of white and then using the Similar command to append all other white areas). Press the Delete key to delete all the selected areas.

5 Alter the opacity of the layer so that more of the original image shows through.

The result should show the original colours, but in a somewhat more muted form. Edges – by using of the Find Edges command – are sharply defined, and in many cases are delineated in black.

Softening effects combined

On page 87 you can see how much more effective the composite *soft focus* effect is compared with the simple Blur tool when used in portraiture. You can extend the same effects – including combinations of grain, blur and others – to nature, as shown here. In conventional photography, less is more can be a useful rule, but here the rule is broken in no uncertain terms by combining *three* filters: Gaussian Blur, Radial Blur and Noise.

2 Begin by creating a duplicate layer. Then apply a modest amount of grain (or noise) to the *background*. The result (with the layer turned off) looks like this.

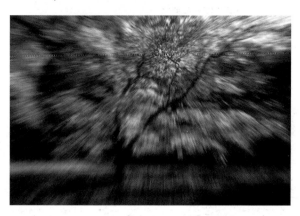

3 Select the layer and apply a Radial Blur filter. Use a modest setting, sufficient to give the highlights a streaked appearance.

1 This autumnal Acer is already quite a pretty image, but you can make it more romantic and etheral..

The lesson from just these two examples is that combined – or modified – filter effects are ultimately more potent than the simple application of a single filter. Regard effects filters as you would any other tool – they are a means to an end, not an end in themselves.

4 Blur the layer slightly using the Gaussian Blur filter and reduce the opacity.

Creating webpage elements/1

Creating your own website was once a difficult task that demanded knowledge of the web's special language, HTML and a raft of relatively complex software. Now, inexpensive applications can be used to build sites that look amazingly professional. In fact, most image editing applications can help conceive and build both web page elements (such as buttons, menus and even animations) and indeed complete web pages.

Buttons

Perhaps the simplest of website navigations is the button. Like conventional buttons, they are designed to be pushed (in this case by clicking with the mouse) and in doing so they respond by changing appearance to take on a 'pressed' look. Infact, you can make such buttons even more responsive by also changing their appearance when the mouse is simply rolled over each: useful as feedback for the user.

Right is how to make a simple button and modify its appearance to take account of different situations.

The step-by-step project on the opposite page shows how to make images sensitive to the actions of a mouse on a web page using the Rollover feature. Rollover is the term given to the image changes and a rollover can be created using a rollover palette. Most image editing applications featuring web page functionality include this feature. In Photoshop, you'll need to switch to ImageReady and use the Rollover palette.

1 Start by drawing a simple shape in a layer. You could use a Marquee tool and fill the selection with a colour, or use a vector tool if your software supports this feature.

2 Give the button some texture by applying a Layer effect (page 100). Bevel and Emboss can be useful here, giving a 3-D illusion and producing a button that looks convincingly three dimensional.

3 Store this image as your 'normal' button.

4 To give the button a highlighted position, so that it is identified when the mouse button passes over, apply an Outer Glow.

5 Save this button as the 'highlighted' form.

6 Finally, to give the impression that the button has been pressed, you could simply alter the lighting angle. By reversing the direction in which light strikes the 'normal' button, you get an instant effect of the button being pressed.

7 For a more sophisticated 'pushed' look, you can alter the contour of the edge bevel. The normal pattern of the bevel you applied to the button's edge is a simple rounded form. By changing this to a more angular form, or perhaps to a compound profile, you get a more interesting effect. Save your final button as the 'pressed' form.

1 Open the normal image and then the Rollover palette. Note that your image will appear in the first frame.

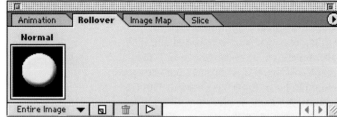

2 Click on the New State icon in the bottom bar of the Rollover palette (indicated by the paper sheet). A new state window appears next to the original, featuring the same image as the original.

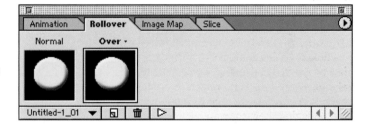

3 Click on this state to make it active. You could now paste in your 'highlighted' image, or apply the same layer effect to the image in this window (any changes you make to the image will apply only to that image). This is called the *Over* Rollover state.

4 Repeat for the third state, this time using the pressed button.

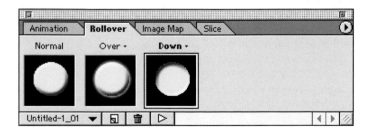

Creating webpage elements/2

Animations

These are created in a similar way as a Rollover – see previous page. You'll sometimes hear them called GIF Animations (and the results Animated GIFs) on account of the use of GIF format images and graphics, rather than the more usual JPEG or TIFF file formats. The GIF format (the name is short for Graphics Interchange Format) was devised specifically for web use and enables a graphic to be made up of animated elements.

Though similar to the type of animation used to create cartoons and other special moving effects, GIF Animations tend to be somewhat simpler. Conventional cartoon animations require every single frame drawn separately, but GIF animations do not. If you have a start and an end point, and if the motion between these two states is logical, such as a square turning into a circle or an object moving across the frame, you can use a special command called Tween to create any number of intermediate frames.

Many image editors include GIF animation routines either as part of the main application, or as an addition. For example, users of PaintShop Pro will find the application Animation Shop ideally suited to the creation of GIF Animations.

Here's how to create a simple animation, in which different shapes appear in the frame, fading in and out. You'll use ImageReady again, this time selecting the Animation palette.

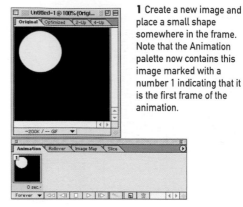

1 Create a new image and place a small shape somewhere in the frame. Note that the Animation palette now contains this image marked with a number 1 indicating that it is the first frame of the animation.

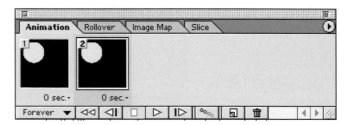

2 Add a second frame (as before, by clicking on the Add Frame icon in the base bar). Nominally, this will contain the same image as the first frame.

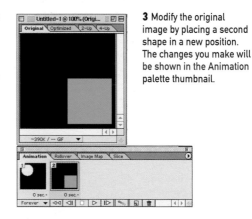

3 Modify the original image by placing a second shape in a new position. The changes you make will be shown in the Animation palette thumbnail.

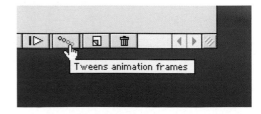

4 Select the Tween command from the menus, or by clicking on the Tween button on the menu bar.

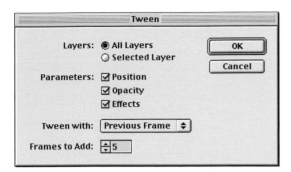

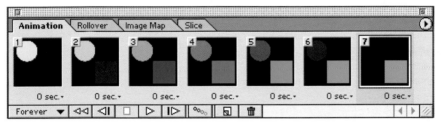

5 The Tween Options palette lets you choose the number of frames inserted between the two existing images and also which elements of the images are interpolated. For example, you can choose Position, Opacities or Effects, either singly, or in combination.

6 After Choosing OK, your Tweened frames will be created and shown in the Animation palette.

Once the frames have been created, you can choose how long each one is displayed. If you have a large number of tweened frames, and choose short display time for each, you get a very smooth animation. Fewer frames and longer intervals give a coarser appearance. You could also choose to have the animation played once, or to play as a specified number of times, or to play continuously. As with Rollover states, you can view the animation 'live' as it would appear on a website, and then make changes if required.

Of course, there is no reason why the technique should be restricted to simple graphics, or to shapes. You could use it, for example, to create rolling slideshows of your images, as below. Save them as GIF files. Note that the GIF format has a restricted, 256-colour palette, making it unsuitable for high-fidelity applications, but it can be switched periodically, or faded.

Digital still and movie photography/1

Film photography clearly distinguishes between still and moving images. In digital imaging, the distinction is not so clear. In the following pages, you can explore how this overlap may be used creatively.

Movies from a digital camera

Digital cameras are adept at capturing still images, but many models can also record movies. To change from still to movie mode, you simply select Movie Mode from the mode select dial, or press the movie button. Movies recorded in this way vary in quality and image size.

Often, images are 320 × 240 pixels and ten frames per second are recorded. This is substantially below that recorded by dedicated digital video cameras, but the quality can still be acceptable for home viewing purposes.

Better still, the file sizes of the movies tend to be very small (depending on the length) and you can even e-mail the files in much the same way as you might ordinary still images. Some (but by no means all) cameras will also record sound with the movie. Again, the quality is OK, but not outstanding.

Movies recorded on digital cameras tend to be regarded (by the camera) as images. You can only record one scene at a time (when you stop recording, the movie file will be stored), and you can review the movie (replaying it, if required) in the camera's playback mode.

The movie files tend to be stored in AVI format, which can be replayed on any computer platform. On Windows computers, the movie will replay using Windows Media Player (or any other that might be set by default); on Macintosh computers, the QuickTime Player plays AVI movies automatically.

The QuickTime player, above, is one of several media players that can be used to replay your movies.

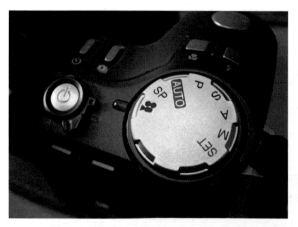

Many digital cameras feature a movie mode. Select the movie icon – as above – and you are ready to begin recording.

QuickTime Pro gives additional flexibility in fine tuning your movie footage.

The QuickTime player is also available (as a free download) for Windows computers and users of either platform can download (at a nominal cost) the 'Pro' version. With this, you can fine tune your video, making adjustments to brightness and colour – and also to treble and bass, if your have also recorded a soundtrack. Perhaps the most interesting possibility offered is that of being able to convert or

transcode your movie file from one format to another.

For example, you could transcode your AVI movie into DV format – the same format as used for recording movies using digital video cameras – and use desktop editing applications to edit your movie scenes into a continuous movie. Often, many of these packages will also allow you to add titles, apply special effects, or even an additional soundtrack.

QuickTime Pro is not restricted to movie applications: you can also create digital slideshows that can then be edited and manipulated just like movies – including adding soundtracks.

Applications such as Movie Maker and iMovie (shown below) can be used to convert your movie files into 'real' movies. You will normally need to convert your AVI movie to DV format (using, for example, QuickTime Pro) in order to create your movie. Special effects (such as sepia toning) can be added at the editing stage.

Digital still and movie photography/2

The arrival of digital video cameras has brought creative opportunities to the video photographer in much the same way as digital stills cameras have empowered the stills photographer. A digital movie camera needn't just be used for movies.

What is a digital video camera?

Digital video cameras have steadily been replacing analogue equipment with smaller cameras and higher quality. And by virtue of being a digital medium, movies can be edited and manipulated in a manner impossible before. Many digital video cameras can offer quality close to that of broadcast-standard cameras. There are three digital video formats:

DV (Digital Video) is the most common with cameras mostly accepting the diminutive miniDV cassettes (larger DV cassettes are used with professional equipment).

Digital8 is a derivative of the popular Video8 and Hi 8 formats introduced by Sony (but adopted by others) during the 1980s, and uses the same tapes as Hi8. Digital8 remains largely a Sony format, but is a useful choice if you have a large back-catalogue of Hi 8 or Video8 tapes – equipment is generally compatible with the older formats. A DV cassette is shown below alongside a Hi8/Digital8 cassette].

MicroMV is also a Sony creation and uses tapes even smaller than MiniDV. The rationale behind MicroMV (other than the creation of even smaller cameras than possible with miniDV) is its encoding method, known as MPEG-2. This is more compact than that used in the other formats, and will take up around half the space on a computer's hard disc.

There are also cameras that write directly to DVDs. Note that any digital video camera requires a digital video output socket to transfer video directly to a computer.

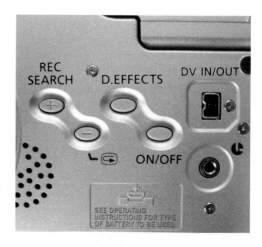

Getting still images direct from your movie camera

Just as many digital stills cameras can take passable movie footage, so many digital video cameras can double up as equally passable stills cameras – but no more than passable. Many digital video cameras are sold as being 'two cameras in one' – but the truth is that because they are designed for different primary functions, discriminating stills photographers will regard them as no more than adequate.

Still images used to be recorded on digital video (DV) cameras by using a Snapshot mode. This records a still image, for perhaps five seconds. Later models have included memory cards (of the same type as found in digital stills cameras) for recording still images 'live'. This gives better image quality and allows the images to be easily downloaded (using, for example, a card reader) in much the same manner as images from a conventional digital camera.

Quality counts: Video cameras are capable of good results, as the image top shows. Only when compared with that from even a modest (2 million pixel) still digital camera, above, does the latter's quality shine through.

Many digital video cameras (such as this MV4 MC model from Canon) include a memory card for the storage of captured still images.

The memory card used for storage on a digital video camera may be a Multimedia Card (shown here) or Secure Digital (SD) Card. If this differs from the card used by your digital camera you may need to buy a second card reader, or a multi-format device.

Tips

- When recording movie footage (whether on a still or movie camera), remember to keep the camera in its conventional landscape mode. Though this sounds obvious, when using a still camera in movie mode there is sometimes a natural inclination to turn the camera and use it in upright (portrait) mode.
- When taking still images with a movie camera, you can disregard the rule above and use portrait or any other creative angle.
- When using movie editing software (such as iMovie, Movie Maker or professional products such as Adobe Premiere) you can combine movie footage with digital still images and extract still images from movie footage – but the quality will be restricted in the same way as noted earlier.

Beyond image manipulation

I mage editing can be compulsive. Before long, your uneasy first steps will be repaid with exciting images. But then what?

Odds are, you'll want to print out your images, for your own pleasure and perhaps to give to family and friends. You'll probably want file copies of your images too, in case the unthinkable happens to your computer. And you'll need to organize your images so that each one in a constantly growing collection can be located with the minimum of effort.

The following pages look at the best ways to protect your collection, and how best to print and display them, including web photo albums.

Saving digital images

When you work repeatedly on the same image or images, it is important to save them correctly. One of the great benefits (or so we are told) of digital images is that they do not degrade no matter what – within reason – you do with them. This is true only up to a point: it really is worth remembering that digital images can degrade merely by saving them.

Most images are saved using the JPEG file format. This is a useful – and portable – storage format that compresses the image file, often substantially. Hence a 12-MB image from a digital camera can be compressed to under 1MB when written to the memory card (without this dodge, even 128MB memory cards would have very limited capacity).

The downside of the JPEG format is that compressing files throws away information. In most cases, loss of image quality is slight, and more than offset by the convenience of small image files. *But,* the degradation is cumulative. Save your images repeatedly, and the effects soon become obvious.

The image on the opposite page (left) was opened and saved (using JPEG compression) five times. The image appears fine, but the damage has started.

After 20 saves, (below left) the image is unusable.

Fortunately, the solution is simple. After you've worked on an image for the first time, save it in a format that does not cause degradation when repeatedly saved. The Tagged Image File Format (TIFF, or TIF) is ideal. It even features an optional compression routine – LZW – that, while not giving the compression of a JPEG, loses nothing – in fact, it's known as *lossless* compression. To prove the point, the image above right and right image was stored as a TIFF and then opened and closed 20 times. There is no degradation.

The drawback is that TIFF files, even using compression, are markedly larger than JPEGs. So you'll still have to decide whether you need quality or to save space. The best advice, usually, is to go for the first. Once quality is lost, no amount of digital manipulation can restore it.

Saving images for display on the web involves a different set of criteria: see page 196.

TIFF original.

Same image after 20 save/open cycles.

Libraries and portfolios

Professional photographers understand only too well the importance of keeping useful records. Being able to find an image quickly is often crucial to one's livelihood. For the amateur, organizing an image collection could seem like a distraction. But no matter how small your collection, it's worth investing time right now into getting it organized. There are plenty of software applications designed to make the task as painless as possible.

Image management software (or Media Asset Management software, as many such applications are now described – acknowledging their ability to manage any media – are nothing more than databases, but a databases with a difference. Most can trawl your hard disc and CDs, find images and automatically build a catalogue. Some (including the well-regarded Piccolo) can even build libraries direct from the images on a camera's memory card. Others, such as Canto's Cumulus and Extensis' Portfolio, have a more traditional approach, behaving like automated library systems.

A typical image management application will give, or ask you to give, each image a unique identifier. Normally this would be a number. Then, a specific title, along with descriptive notes (such as when and where the shot was taken, exposure details and any other relevant comments). You might also use a field that describes the images' source, such as scanner, digital camera and so on.

Finally, the software will ask for two key bits of information. First, keywords: these attach to the image and help to search for it later. For example, a photograph of The White House might have keywords *President, Government, Washington and Federal*. Should you wish to search for all your images relating to U.S. federal government, or the presidency, this image would appear among them.

A screen shot from Canto Cumulus, showing how the software presents all images as thumbnails. Above and above left, examples of images catalogued by Extensis's Portfolio.

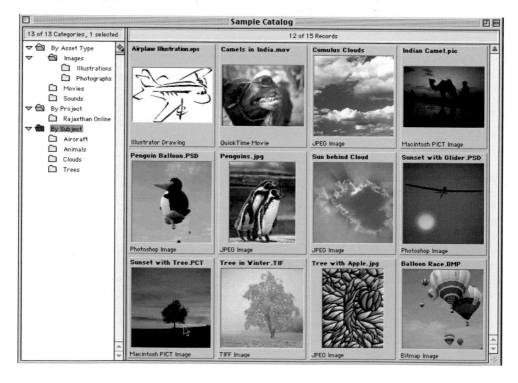

192

Lastly, you will be asked to define the location of the image: the physical place where it can be found.

If all this sounds tedious – well, you'll find it tedious; but it's no less important for that. Some applications try to take the slog out of it by assigning many of the non-specific details automatically. Groups can be created, and given keywords, rather than having to annotate each individually; locations can be automatically identified (and, should you move the image, say from hard disc to CD, will be automatically

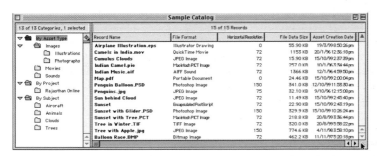

tracked). Potentially a life-saver. So you could find that the amount of information you have to enter is refreshingly small, after all. And it won't take you long to realize how valuable this investment of time and patience has been.

Applications such as Canto Cumulus present all media (including movie and sound files) as thumbnails. Clicking on any thumbnail will – assuming the source file is currently on the computer – open that file for closer inspection. Switching to list mode

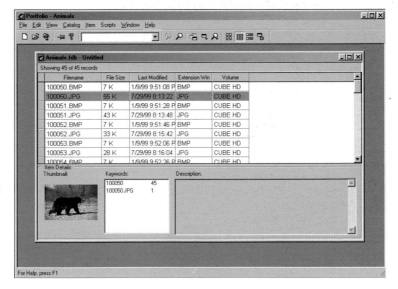

gives more information about each image, presented as a text table. Note the catalogue's structure, displayed in the panel to the left.

Extensis's Portfolio is one of several applications that will search your hard disc for images and load them into a catalogue automatically. Only minor remedial work is

then required to complete the album. Portfolio is a useful application because it is available in different versions, depending on the size of your image library. It is easy to expand at a later date from (say) the personal desktop version to a full server version that would give you professional image library capability..

Commercial printing services

One of the great bonuses of digital photography is its immediacy. You can take a photo and print a quality A4 print within minutes. But though inkjet prints are of a quality that rivals the best in traditional photoprocessing, there are times when only a photographic print will do. For these situations – and when you need a product such as a T-shirt printed with a photo – a range of photo-finishing services is available.

Many high street photolabs can now accept digital images (direct from digital cameras, SmartMedia or CompactFlash cards, or from CD or disc) and create artwork. Normally, the images are copied from your original card or disc, so you needn't worry about losing the original. Many of these facilities can also create photos using the same high-speed processors as on offer to users of conventional film, so your photos may be ready for collection in less than an hour.

Online processing services are becoming increasingly popular. Photo sites (for example, Shutterfly.com, Bootsphoto.com, Jessops.com) encourage you to upload images from your computer to the web and offer a range of printing services, from conventional 6 × 4 inch prints through to poster-sized prints and giftware. Within a few days, your work is delivered by mail or ready for collection at your local store.

Some of these sites offer a complete service that includes elementary online image editing tools (so you can perform minor corrections 'live') and may also provide expert help to repair damaged images. Of course, such services cost extra.

Topfoto (topfotoservices.com) can produce prints and a wide selection of photo gifts from both traditional and digital images.

Online processing services may also produce greetings or birthday cards from your images. Though inkjet printers (along with the templates supplied with many image editors – see page 000) can produce good results, nothing beats a professionally finished product.

The only drawback to online services is the need to provide quality images. If you have a slow or poor Internet connection, this could prove expensive.

Printing at home

In the digital darkroom, it's the printer that provides the same moment of magic as the print processor in the traditional darkroom. Slowly but surely, the print emerges and all your hard work is finally there in tangible form.

There's a big choice of printers, so how do you know which is for you? They fall into three categories: inkjet, dye sublimation, thermal and laser.

Inkjet printers are the most common, and although not all are capable of printing to photographic standards, they provide a

Shutterfly (shutterfly.com) offers a range of services when you upload digital images to the site.

Services such as Shutterfly are excellent for producing personalised stationery, including greetings cards such as these Christmas cards. Simple step-by-step instructions let you combine your photo with a choice of layouts and embellishments. Shutterfly will even mail the cards directly to third parties.

reasonably economic solution to all home and home office printing needs. If you intend to do a significant amount of photo printing, ensure that your chosen model is capable of photo-realistic printing. These models often feature *six* ink colours, where light magenta and light cyan are added to the normal set. You'll also find models capable of printing over the entire page (i.e. with no margin); that accept paper from rolls as well as in sheet form; and some will print to sizes larger than A3.

The cost of new cartridges for inkjet printers can mount up, particularly if you often print to A3, and some can be very choosy about the paper required for photographic-quality prints. But as they can also be used for more mundane work, such as printing your day to day correspondence, they are a good buy. Look out, too, for models that offer inks with a permanence rating better than 20 or even 100 years. Though it's hard to substantiate such claims, if you value your work, you need to give it the best chance of survival.

Dye sublimation printers are somewhat more expensive than inkjet and capable of true photographic quality. They aren't suitable for other printing activities. Dye-subs work by vaporising a solid dye directly on to the paper. As the colour is not liquefied at any stage, prints emerge completely dry and ready to use. Special transfer sheets impregnated with black, cyan, magenta and yellow dye are required and these can be costly. The receptor paper can be expensive, too. The benefit comes in image quality that is often the best you could expect without resorting to true photographic processes.

Thermal printers, such as Thermal Autochrome, or TA, are often grouped with dye subs, although they work differently. TA printers use specialized papers embedded with dyes. The print moves over a heated print head that, according to temperature, releases the dyes. The print needs to pass through the printer three times to release the three colours. Quality is high, but so are running costs, and they work slowly.

Laser printers offer speed. Colour laser copiers are far faster than most other printers even if the quality – at best – is only equal to an average photo-realistic inkjet. Given the high purchase price and high toner costs, laser printers are not a viable option for domestic users.

Printer type	Photo quality Inkjet	DyeSub/thermal	Laser
Printer cost	Low-moderate	Moderate	High
Ink/Consumables cost	High	High	Moderate
Image caption	Good	Very good	Average to good
Image permanence	Very good	Very good	OK
Speed	Slow	Slower	Fast

Your photos and the web

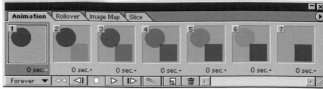

A GIF animation is easily created in applications such as Adobe's ImageReady or Jasc's Animation Shop.

It is a testament to the rise and rise of the Internet that all the best image manipulation applications now include web-compatible features. Some offer simple web photo album creation, while some can be used to create entire web pages, ready for the net.

Saving images for the web

Image editing and manipulation processes are, for the most part, identical whether your image will ultimately be printed, displayed on a web page or e-mailed. But how you save an image will be different.

When you want to save an image on your computer for printing or editing, you need to retain as much quality as possible. A printed image of 200 dots per inch sized to A4 will be more than 100MB. To send an image of this size by e-mail would be totally impractical. Even those using the fastest broadband connections would balk at the time needed to transmit. To distribute images to the web, you need files sizes as small as possible, without loss of quality.

This is done through the process known as *Optimization*, which involves saving the image in a web-savvy format, compressing the image and, where possible, reducing the number of colours.

For everyday digital imaging, TIFF and JPEG file formats (see page 000) have their drawbacks: compressing an image removes information and introduces artefacts. But for the web, they are very useful because a degree of information loss is acceptable in exchange for a compact file that will load quickly. In any case, images for the web have relatively small dimensions; and, as computer screens show only 72 dots per inch, there's little to be gained by saving them to a higher resolution.

In fact, there are two file formats that can be used to optimize web images: GIF and PNG. GIF – Graphics Interchange

Format – supports only 256 colours, so may not be appropriate for many images (though it is ideal for graphics). GIF files can be modestly compressed, by around 40 per cent, but they are lossless – ie there is no degradation. Such files can also support transparencies and animation, making them ideally suited to the web. The simple rotating logo-type animations seen on websites are often GIF animations.

PNG – Portable Networks Graphics – is a relatively new format that suffers (in common with many such newcomers) from not being supported by all web browsers. Again, the format works by modest compression, but a greater number of colours can be used than with xxxxxxxxx.

Because optimization involves colour reduction and compression, most applications offer the opportunity to preview images with several optimization states along with the original. Often, you will be advised on how that image will download, both visually and in terms of download time.

Above is the optimization screen in ImageReady, showing the original image and three optimization states (below the image). Note that the predicted download

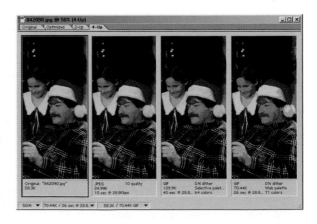

time is also shown in each case. You can use these surrogate images to observe the effect of compression and, where necessary, to alter the parameters to get the best balance between quality and download time. In this example, even the heavily compressed JPEG image (second from left) is acceptable; but both the GIF images (third and fourth from left) are compromised, the last especially so.

In applications not designed specifically with web graphics in mind, you might find a more rudimentary feature called Save for Web. When using a command such as this, you may not have the multiscreen comparison feature.

A photo gallery for the web

It is easy to create a photo gallery in which to display your photographic prowess on the Internet. Photoshop Elements has a fully automated tool for this purpose, and is typical of similar features offered elsewhere.

The big bonus of automated systems such as this is that they take away virtually all the guess work about image optimisation and shield you from having to write HTML – the web's own programming language.

Here's how to create your own online photo gallery:

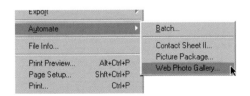

1 Gather together all the images you want to include in the site in a single folder. It helps if you give them a short name and a number.

2 Select File>Automate>Web Gallery to open the Web Gallery dialogue.

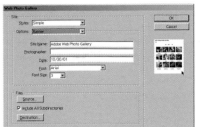

3 Choose a format for the web gallery (a limited selection is supplied). Also choose a title, and add your own name if you wish. Select your source folder (that containing the images) and a destination folder, where the web gallery will be saved when generated.

4 Select OK to start creating the gallery: this may take some time – you'll see progress on screen.

5 Preview your web gallery. It will appear in your default web browser.

6 Note how both the images and the captions are active links. Click on either, and the selected image will appear.

7 Post the gallery to your website. If you do not have a website, contact your Internet service provider, who will give you details about creating one and uploading files.

Web gallery tips

- Choose the names for the shots carefully – they will be used as captions.
- Be careful with numbers, too. They will be used to order the sequence of shots (precede the numbers 1 to 9 with a '0' to prevent '2', for example, being listed after 11, 12, 13...)

Onwards and upwards

If you've been excited this far, where do you go now? Don't worry, there's plenty more...

...Websites

Extending your skills to creating a complete website doesn't demand much. Like it or not, the Internet is the best showcase for your work. Having a web presence is not as daunting as it was.

... 3D graphics

Now that even mid-ranged home computers virtually have computing power to spare, three-dimensional graphics applications will run successfully on most machines. With some programs, such as Corel's excellent

Above, Bryce is equally at home creating believable landscapes, alien worlds or elements of digital images.

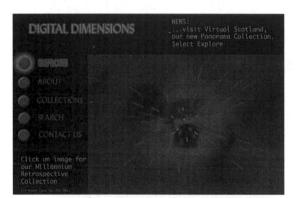

Left and below, this home page for Digital Dimensions digital panoramas website was created in Photoshop in around half an hour and – given half an hour more – was made 'active' with links to the other pages on the site.

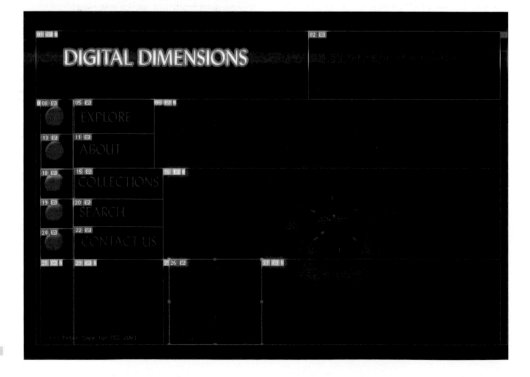

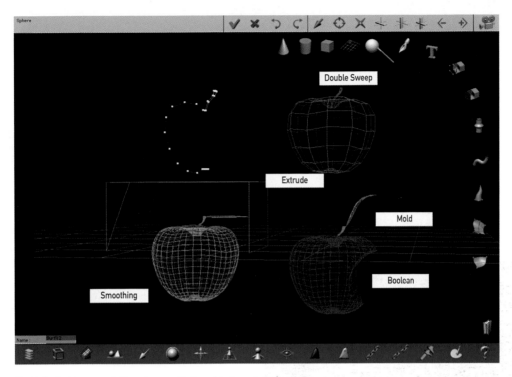

Create fantastic – or realistic – shapes with Amapi Software's 3D package

(if idiosyncratic) Bryce, you can render landscapes, skyscapes and more. Use these either to create novel worlds, or to provide landscape details that can be combined (in your imaging software) with your own images to produce fantastic landscapes.

Other applications, such as Amapi 3D, enable you to design virtually any 3D shapes and then convert ('render') them into realistic forms, complete with the expected lighting effects.

...Digital video

It is not as big a step as you might think to move from still digital images to digital movies. Easy-to-use software such as iMovie and MovieMaker has transformed moviemaking, enabling anyone to get interesting results with minimal effort or training.

There is a surprising degree of similarity between still and movie editing: many effects you employ on your photos can be applied to movies, too. You can even add digital still shots to movies either for effect

or to create movie slide shows that can be distributed on tape.

Whether you choose to stick to digital image manipulation, or to use your experiences as a springboard into new worlds, we wish you well. Just remember: it can be addictive.

Simple Drag and Drop functionality makes digital movie making simple.

Websites and books

Image editing websites

www.adobe.com

www.photoshop-cafe.com

www.mccannas.com/pshop/menu.htm

www.plugins.com/plugins/photoshop

www.corel.com

www.jasc.com

www.ulead.com

www.mgisoft.com

www.alienskin.com

www.andromeda.com

www.fractal.com

www.extensis.com

www.xaostools.com

Further Reading

50 Fast Digital Photo Techniques

Gregory Georges, Hungry Minds New York, 2001

How to do Everything with Photoshop Elements

Molly Joss, Osborne/McGraw Hill Berkeley CA, 2001

Adobe Photoshop 6 Digital Darkroom

Lisa Lee, Prima Publishing Rosewood (CA), 2001

Adobe Photoshop 6.0 for Photographers

Martin Evening, Focal Press Oxford, 2001

CorelDRAW 10: The Official Guide

Steve Bain, Osborne McGraw-Hill, Berkeley CA, 2000

Paintshop Pro 7 in Easy Steps

Stephen Copestake, Computer Step, Southam (Warwickshire UK), 2001

Paintshop Pro 7 Explained

N. Kantaris, Bernard Babani Publishing)
Ltd London, June 2001

Photo-Paint 10

Dave Huss, Osborne McGraw-Hill,
BerkeleyCA, November 2000

Silver Pixels

Tom Ang, Argentum London, 1999

The Digital Photography Handbook

Simon Joinson, Metro Books London, 1998
(reprinted 2001)

The Photoshop Users A to Z

Peter Cope, Thames and Hudson
London, 2001

Complete Guide to Digital Photography

Michael Freeman, Silver Pixel Press
Rochester NY, 2001

Glossary

Cross references are indicated by italics.

Airbrush Tool

Digital equivalent of the artist's airbrush. Sprays a soft-edge line with the *foreground colour*, with the size and opacity determined by the *brush* and *opacity* settings respectively.

Aliased, anti-aliased

The rough, jagged edge of diagonal and curved images displayed on a computer screen (or printed), caused by the *pixel*-based nature of the images. Images affected in this way are known as aliased. Anti-aliasing is used to smooth transitions by adding pixels of intermediate colour.

Artefact

Any flaw in an image due to electronic effects during taking, processing or later handling. The most common include those due to image compression and zebra striping visible in dark areas of night shots.

Background colour

The colour revealed when image elements are removed from a scene and the end point of a colour *gradient*.

Bezier curve

A mathematically determined line used to create paths. The line can be manipulated (to follow an object boundary, for example) by dragging anchor point *handles*.

Bit depth

Also known as bits per pixel. A value that determines the colour (or grey) value of an image. The greater the number, the more greys and colours that can define the colours in an image.

Blur filters

Filters designed to unfocus an image or an image selection. Often used to increase depth of field or to soften the edges of a selection.

Brush

A definition of the size and shape of the painting effect employed by a painting tool such as the *Airbrush* or paintbrush.

Clipboard

Area of temporary storage in a computer's memory designed to hold selections made using the cut or copy commands.

Colour swatches

A set of colours that can be selected for painting. Can comprise preset colours or include colours used regularly by the user and sampled using the *eyedropper tool*. Usually collected together in a *palette*.

Crop tool

Selection tool used to define the area of an image to be retained. The area outside is discarded.

Eyedropper tool

Used to sample a specific colour from an image. Once sampled, that colour becomes the current *foreground colour* and could optionally be saved as a *colour swatch*.

Fill tool

Sometimes called the Paint Bucket, this is a tool used to flood a selection with the current *foreground colour*.

Foreground colour

The colour used to paint with when a painting tool is selected.

GIF format

File format used to save (principally) graphic files used on the web.

Gradient tool

Enables a smooth transition between at least two colours or one colour and *transparency*. Normally, a gradient is created between the *foreground* and *background* colours.

Greyscale

Displays an image in black, white and 254 intermediate shades of grey.

Handles

Small boxes found at the corners and midpoints of the sides of selections. Depending on the feature, these can be used for resizing, distorting or rotating the selection. A basic tool of digital imaging.

Hue/saturation

Command used to alter the hue (the colour) of an image and the saturation (the intensity of the colour).

JPEG format

File format used for saving image files, noted for its ability to compress images. Compressed images do, however, suffer from artefacts and degradation.

Layer

A virtual plane in an image that can be painted on or manipulated without affecting those above or below. Specialized layers (called Adjustment Layers in some applications) are transparent, but modify the underlying layers in terms of colour, contrast or other variables. Called *Objects* in some applications.

Marquee tool

Selection tool that bases the selection on regular rectangular, elliptical or (occasionally) other regular geometric forms.

Mask

Strictly, a term used to describe a coating applied to part of an image in order to prevent it being affected by manipulations and edits. Also used to describe part of an image that is not actively selected.

Move tool

Tool used to move a selection to a new position or move the contents of a layer relative to the contents of other layers.

Object

See *Layer*.

Opacity

Also known as *Transparency*. A feature of layers and effects that enables them to be rendered opaque or transparent or somewhere in between (and usually expressed as a percentage).

Paint bucket tool

See *Fill tool*.

Palette

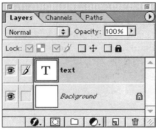

An interface element containing controls or settings for a particular tool or command. Unlike dialogue boxes, which appear only when required, palettes are usually visible continuously (subject to context and whether a Show/Hide Palette command has been used). Palettes can often be moved freely around the screen or 'docked' conveniently.

Pixel

Fundamental component of a digital image

Quick mask

A *Mask* applied using painting tools to aid in object selection.

Selection

Part of an image (or the entire image) on which manipulations, edits and transformations can take place. It is the active area. Areas outside it are describes as unselected or *masked*.

Stroke

When an object selection is stroked, a line is applied to the selection boundary (colour and thickness can be determined by the user).

Transparency

See *Opacity*.

Vector image

Images comprising vector elements, ie, those determined by mathematical expressions rather than *pixels*.

Index

Pages 22,23: Illustrations of Apple Studio display and iMac courtesy of Apple Computer Inc.

Pages 18, 19: Photographs courtesy of Hasselblad, Nikon.

Corel Corporation for the use of their images throughout this book.

ArcSoft Corporation, Shutterfly, MGI Software (UK) for use of collateral relating to their products and websites.

Special thanks to my children, David and Sarah, for their patience in being used as unpaid models
in many of the specially commissioned shots used here.